SERMON ON THE MOUNT

FIELD GUIDE
FOR YOUR FAITH

JOHN RANDALL

CALVARY

Calvary Chapel San Juan Capistrano, 31612 El Camino Real, San Juan Capistrano, CA 92675

SERMON ON THE MOUNT: FIELD GUIDE FOR YOUR FAITH

By John Randall

A Daily Walk Publishing
31612 El Camino Real
San Juan Capistrano, CA 92675
949-443-2572

www.adailywalk.org

ISBN 978-1-7328933-1-3

Unless otherwise indicated, all Scripture quotations are taken from the following Bible translations with ESV sourced in brackets:

New King James Version of the Bible. Copyright © 1982 by Thomas Nelson, Inc. Used by permission. All rights reserved.

Scripture quotations are from the ESV® Bible (The Holy Bible, English Standard Version®), copyright © 2001 by Crossway, a publishing ministry of Good News Publishers. Used by permission. All rights reserved.

Translation emendations, amplifications, and paraphrases are by the author.

Cover Design: Hollow Cobos and Zach Ruiz
Cover/Interior Layout: John Shaffer
Photography: www.COBOS.co
Editor: Allie Bullock Kagamaster

Printed in the United States of America

CONTENTS

INTRODUCTION

I t was the late biblical scholar and preacher A. T. Robertson, who said the "Sermon on the Mount" stands out as the greatest single sermon of all time in its pointedness and power. I believe that the "Sermon on the Mount" is a sermon that the church desperately needs today.

In many ways, Christianity has become increasingly shallow. Perhaps part of the blame is to be laid at the feet of us who are pastors. We have a biblical mandate to present, preach, and proclaim God's Word. Yet, in many pulpits today and in platforms around the country preaching has been reduced to pep talks about how to have a better life or to better yourself instead of getting right with God. And in some places, we have less scripture and more anecdotes. More personal stories, less biblical content. We have more theatrical presentations and illustrations rather than a solid exposition of the Bible. And if we're not careful, it can be reduced to a show to entertain instead of a church to equip the saints for the work of the ministry.

Without the substance of the Scriptures, people are unaware of what it truly means to be a Christian. If we're not accurately preaching the Word, then we could be guilty of bringing people into a false sense of security. And that is why the Bible says, "Let not many of you become teachers knowing you will receive a stricter judgment from the Lord."

This is a serious thing we do in the presentation of God's Word. Perhaps we could also point the finger at ourselves individually. We're so easily distracted, aren't we, in our culture? We've grown accustomed to and are trained to have the information we want in seconds to the point that our attention span is so limited that we don't seek the Lord, don't have time to wait on the Lord. We don't have time to sink our roots deep in prayer or the study of God's Word. We have so many other things that are a priority in life that a relationship of deeper significance with the Saviour can become less important. Jesus can become more of an acquaintance, someone we know about, rather than someone we intimately know; or worse, He can become a stranger.

So what then does it mean to be a Christian? What does it mean to be a disciple? What does it mean to walk with the Lord? Does it mean that I simply go to church once a week or does this relationship with God affect how I live?

When you read and study the "Sermon on the Mount," these questions are answered, but it's important to keep a few things in mind. First of all, this sermon does not teach us what to do to be saved. Rather, this sermon speaks to those who are already saved and instructs them on how to live. This sermon is for every Christian and is a message for true believers. For those who desire to be like Jesus, who want to live for Jesus. This isn't a sermon one reads and falsely assumes is just for the super saint or for a pastor of a church or a missionary on a mission field. The "Sermon on the Mount" is a message for every single child of God, every single person who calls themselves a Christian.

Second, the exhortations given and the characteristics mentioned within the sermon are not to be viewed as optional, meaning we read the Words of Jesus and accept what we feel comfortable with and then reject and disregard what we find uncomfortable. Regardless of how we feel in reading the Words of Christ, all of it is to be applied and obeyed.

Third, none of these descriptions refers to (especially in the first twelve verses) what we would call a natural tendency. Each description listed requires the power of the Holy Spirit attached to our lives to live according to the things that Jesus says. I can't emphasize that enough! And this is why: often people say, "Well, I don't go to church, and I don't necessarily call myself a Christian, but I live by the Words of Jesus." But the truth is we don't naturally conform to the description given in the Beatitudes and the rest of the "Sermon on the Mount." We can't apply what Jesus is saying apart from the power of the Holy Spirit. So, as we approach this sacred text, we do so with a real sense of humility.

We are prone to judge or critique some sermons. I have done this myself with my sermons. We might say things like "Well, that was an OK sermon" or "I didn't like that sermon" or as a pastor, I might say, "That's the worse sermon I've ever given."

We can critique some sermons, but the "Sermon on the Mount" critiques us. This sermon reveals what's in our hearts. In light of this fact, we must approach this sermon with great humility, a sense of honesty and a willingness to change our perspective on how we see things to the perspective of Christ and the way He sees things.

We begin first of all by looking at the Gospel of Matthew 4:23-25 to set the backdrop for this particular message of Christ: "And Jesus went about all Galilee, teaching in their synagogues, preaching the gospel of the kingdom, and healing all kinds of sickness and all kinds of disease among the people. Then His fame went throughout all Syria, and they brought to Him all sick people who were afflicted with various diseases and torments, and those who were demon-possessed, epileptics, and paralytics; and He healed them. Great multitudes followed Him—from Galilee, and Decapolis, Jerusalem, Judea, and beyond the Jordan."

At this point, Jesus' ministry was fulltime. Matthew describes His three-point approach, which consisted of: teaching in the synagogue, preaching the gospel of the Kingdom, and healing those who were sick. His ministry had been in Capernaum, Nazareth, and Cana. Now, He expanded His ministry into the surrounding towns and villages. According to one historian, there were an estimated 200 villages at this time around the Galilee region, and Jesus was visiting all of these other places, as Matthew 4:25 states. Matthew mentions these accounts 49 times within his gospel, highlighting the large crowds and great multitudes that surrounded Jesus.

People followed Jesus for different reasons. Some came to Jesus for healing or to hear Him teach. Others showed up to partake of the food He provided on various occasions, while some like the religious leaders came to criticize, to find something wrong with Jesus. But as He was teaching and preaching, He emphasized that the Kingdom of God—also referred to as the Kingdom of Heaven—was at hand.

Naturally, the question on the minds of the people was how to enter into this kingdom of which He spoke. They wanted to know if they were righteous enough to enter into His kingdom. The people knew from the Old Testament scriptures that righteousness was indeed a requirement for acceptance into God's Kingdom. They knew the words of the psalmist in Psalm 24, for instance, who said, "Only those who have clean hands and a pure heart can approach this kingdom," so they came inquiring of Jesus concerning the righteousness required to gain entrance into His Kingdom.

So it is with this backdrop that the "Sermon on the Mount" opens.

1

THE JOYFUL DISCIPLE

"Seeing the crowds, he went up on the mountain, and when he sat down, his disciples came to him. And he opened his mouth and taught them, saying: 'Blessed are the poor in spirit, for theirs is the kingdom of heaven'" (Matthew 5:1-3 ESV).

J esus addressed the concerns of the people. He knew the questions on their minds. And so He went up onto a mountain, and when He sat down, His disciples gathered around Him as He began to teach. There is a difference between the multitudes and the disciples. What does it mean to be a disciple?

In the New Testament, the Greek word for disciple—*mathetes*—means "more than just a student or a learner." A disciple is a follower who adheres completely to the teachings of another, making it the rule of his life and conduct. Jesus shared with the multitudes about the cost of discipleship. Later on, Jesus told the crowds, "If anyone desires to come after me, let him deny himself, take up his cross, and follow me" (Matthew 16:24 ESV). This is what Jesus meant for someone to become a disciple.

There were those who heard what Jesus said and what it meant to follow Him, but there came a point when some actually ended up leaving Him. John tells us: "After this many of his disciples turned back and no longer walked with him" (John 6:66 ESV). In Luke's gospel, Jesus said to those gathered around Him: "Why do you call me Lord, Lord and don't do the things which I say?" (Luke 6:46 ESV).

Here Jesus is talking about what it means to be a disciple, to truly follow Him with a firm commitment. Jesus used the term "disciple" but never used the term "Christian." The first instance of the word "Christian" is found in the Book of Acts 11:26: "And the disciples were first called Christians in Antioch. The term "Christian" (belonging to Christ) was a derogatory term. The only other two times the word "Christian" appears in the New Testament is in Acts 26:28, "Then Agrippa said to Paul, "You almost persuade me to become a Christian," and in 1 Peter 4:16, "Yet if anyone suffers as a Christian, let him not be ashamed, but let him glorify God in this matter."

Biblically speaking, a Christian is a disciple of Christ, a follower of Jesus. A Christian is someone who has placed their faith in the Lord Jesus Christ. The Bible says a Christian has been born again by the Holy Spirit. A Christian belongs to Christ and is daily being transformed into the image or likeness of Christ as they follow Him. This is not talking about a life of perfection but about someone who is in pursuit of, and following after Jesus Christ. Are you in pursuit of the Lord today? The question is: How many people claim to be Christian in name only? If put on trial for Christianity, would there be enough evidence to convict those who claim they are followers of Jesus Christ?

In our cultural Christian environment, it is easy for people to claim Christianity yet not live as a Christian. A true Christian is not one who is a Christian in name only. A true Christian is actively a disciple of Jesus Christ. Jesus told His disciples to go out into the world and make disciples followers of Christ. This was the Great Commission. A Christian, therefore, is one who has counted the cost and is committed to following Jesus, accepting the call to go wherever the Lord leads. The Christian disciple adheres to the teaching of Christ, makes Christ the first priority in life and lives accordingly. Their activities involve helping others understand what it means to follow Christ. The true Christian disciple is a believer in Christ, embracing the new life in Christ, and is filled with the indwelling of the Holy Spirit. The true Christian loves Jesus and is obedient to His commands.

Paul described the reality of life as a disciple in Galatians 2:20: "I have been crucified with Christ; it is no longer I who live, but Christ lives in me; and the life which I now live in the flesh I live by faith in the Son of God, who loved me and gave Himself for me."

This is what it means to be a Christian. Therefore, attending church, taking holy communion or baptism at birth does not automatically make a person a Christian. A person must come into Christianity by faith. In John 3, Jesus said, "Most assuredly, I say to you, unless one is born again, he cannot see the kingdom of God" (v. 3), and "Do not marvel that I said to you, 'You must be born again'" (v. 7).

A disciple accepts Christ as Lord and Savior and then follows after Him.

2

THE BEATITUDES

Seeing the crowds, he went up on the mountain, and when he sat down, his disciples came to him. And he opened his mouth and taught them, saying:

'Blessed are the poor in spirit, for theirs is the kingdom of heaven.

Blessed are those who mourn, for they shall be comforted.

Blessed are the meek, for they shall inherit the earth.

Blessed are those who hunger and thirst for righteousness, for they shall be satisfied.

Blessed are the merciful, for they shall receive mercy.

Blessed are the pure in heart, for they shall see God.

Blessed are the peacemakers, for they shall be called sons of God.

Blessed are those who are persecuted for righteousness' sake, for theirs is the kingdom of heaven.

Blessed are you when others revile you and persecute you and utter all kinds of evil against you falsely on my account. Rejoice and be glad, for your reward is great in heaven, for so they persecuted the prophets who were before you' (Matthew 5:1-12 ESV).

The "Sermon on the Mount" begins with the Beatitudes. There is a difference of opinion as to the actual number of beatitudes. The Bible lists at least eight. That is eight declarations of blessings spoken by Jesus. Each "beatitude" begins with the word "blessed," or "oh, how happy," which implies inner satisfaction—a sufficiency not dependent upon outward circumstances and more than superficial happiness. Instead, if we desire to live a blessed life with the joy of the Lord, a certain attitude will follow with characteristics that are part of the Kingdom of God.

There is a difference between happiness and joy. People long for Happiness. In the American Bill of Rights, we have the right to pursue happiness and desire to do the things that give us a happy life. But happiness is often determined upon how one feels, on present circumstances, or material possessions. People achieve happiness by what they are involved in, how they feel, and financial status.

On the other hand, joy is something people experience despite circumstances or feelings. Joy is the work of the Holy Spirit. The Bible says, "Do not sorrow, for the joy of the Lord is your strength" (Nehemiah 8:10).

What makes a person happy? What does a person hope for to create happiness? Whatever that might be, happiness can come and go with sadness or sorrow. But the good news is that one day we will be in the presence of the Lord and there will be no more sadness. The Bible tells us, "You will show me the path of life; in Your presence is fullness of joy; at your right hand are pleasures forevermore" (Psalm 16:11).

The Beatitudes taught by Jesus to His disciples is a list of characteristics, eight declarations of blessings to be found in the lives of those following Christ in response to obedience to His Word.

THE FIRST BEATITUDE: POVERTY OF SPIRIT

Blessed are the poor in spirit,
for theirs is the Kingdom of Heaven.

The first beatitude addresses a proper perspective toward oneself, honesty about who we really are. To be "poor in spirit" is a confession that in our natural state, we are void of "spiritual assets," sinful and rebellious and utterly without moral virtues adequate to commend ourselves to God. Poor in spirit does not refer to self-hatred. Those poor in spirit have a proper perspective of themselves and recognize their utter spiritual bankruptcy before God. The poor in spirit admit that due to sin, they are completely destitute spiritually and do not have the resources to save themselves.

As the psalmist said, "But I am poor and needy; yet the Lord thinks upon me. You are my help and my deliverer; Do not delay, O my God" (Psalm 40:17), the poor in spirit relies on God for salvation.

The Apostle Paul wrote: "For I know that in me (that is, in my flesh) nothing good dwells; for to will is present with me, but how to perform what is good I do not find" (Romans 7:18), and, "As it is written: There is none righteous, no, not one; there is none who seeks after God. They have all turned aside; they have together become unprofitable; there is none who does good, no, not one" (Romans 3:10-12). And Jesus said, "I am the vine, you are the branches. He who abides in Me, and I in him, bears much fruit; for without Me you can do nothing" (John 15:5). Entrance to the Kingdom opens up to us and becomes ours when we realize that we truly cannot save ourselves without the Lord.

Spiritual poverty, as well as all the beatitudes, represents the antithesis to present world standards, which say the exact opposite of what Jesus said. The world offers a much different message. The world preaches that a person must love themselves, have self-esteem, develop a better self-image, and focus on self-realization as a prescription to cure all of their ills. Yet in reality, self-absorption can make one miserable. We are urged by social norms to develop a love of self and self-importance to fill our poverty of spirit. However, self-realization reveals ongoing spiritual emptiness. As Paul wrote in Romans, our flesh wars against the spirit bringing forth sin and separation from God. "O wretched man that I am! Who will deliver me from this body of death? I thank God—through Jesus Christ, our Lord! So then, with the mind, I myself serve the law of God, but with the flesh the law of sin" (Romans 7:24-25).

Isaiah realized his place when he saw the Lord on His throne, "high and lifted up, and the train of His robe [filling] the temple" (Isaiah 6:1); his response was humble: "Woe is me, for I am undone! Because I am a man of unclean lips, And I dwell in the midst of a people of unclean lips; For my eyes have seen the King, The Lord of hosts" (Isaiah 6:5). Isaiah saw himself not in light of somebody else, but in light of the Lord. When we look at Jesus, we realize our poverty in spirit.

Another example of spiritual poverty is found in the Book of Joshua when he encountered the commander of the army of the Lord (Joshua 5:13-15). Then there was Daniel, who when he saw the Lord in a vision, lost all strength (Daniel 10:8). Simon Peter witnessed something similar when Jesus challenged him to put the boat back in the water. "When Simon Peter saw it, he fell down at Jesus' knees, saying, 'Depart from me, for I am a sinful man, O Lord!'" (Luke 5:8).

These accounts illustrate the true meaning of poverty in spirit. We are blessed when we are poor in spirit because the promise given to the poor in spirit is the Kingdom of God. The Kingdom of Heaven opens up to us when we come to realize that we fall short before a Holy God.

But why do people choose to reject Christ? Pride is one of the biggest roadblocks for people to come to the Lord. The idea that we are good enough prevents us from entering into His Kingdom, and its doors will remain shut until we come to the place of humility. The poor in spirit are humble before God, and the Bible tells us He responds to this. God resists the proud but gives grace to the humble.

"Therefore, submit to God. Resist the devil, and he will flee from you. Draw near to God, and He will draw near to you" (James 4:6-7). James 4:10 gives us a promise for when we come to the Lord in humility: "Humble yourselves in the sight of the Lord, and He will lift you up." He's not going to turn anyone away. "A bruised reed He will not break, and a smoking flax He will not quench;" (Isaiah 42:3).

Concerning poverty in spirit, the third stanza of lyrics from the "Rock of Ages" hymn powerfully illustrates this message:

> Nothing in my hand I bring,
> Simply to thy cross I cling;
> Naked, come to thee for dress,
> Helpless, look to thee for grace;
> Foul, I to the Fountain fly;
> Wash me, Saviour, or I die.

What, then, is the promise? What is the blessing for the one who is poor in spirit? Notice the Bible says, "For theirs is the Kingdom of God." This may seem like a paradox for when we think about being poor, it means having nothing. But Heaven's economy is much different than our economy. Paul's epistle to the Philippians, written thirty years after his conversion at a time when he had lost everything articulates this attitude of poverty in spirit (Philippians 3:7-11).

In a worldly perspective, Paul had everything. Everything you could want. Yet he realized when he was introduced to Jesus how poverty-stricken he really was. There were many things that at one point, he thought valuable and priceless, but when he gave his life to Christ, these things became meaningless compared with the righteousness of Christ. James 2:5 confirms the value of spiritual poverty with a question: "Has God not chosen the poor of this world to be rich in faith and heirs of the kingdom which He promised to those who love Him?" Jesus gave a vivid illustration of one who demonstrated the poverty of spirit. In Luke's gospel, Jesus spoke of an earthly story with a heavenly meaning (Luke 18:9-14).

The tax collector knew he was a sinner, bankrupt in spirit and in need of a savior, and all he could say was, "Lord, be merciful to me." Mercy is getting what you don't deserve, but when he asked God for mercy, Jesus said, he went home justified, forgiven, and right in the sight of the Lord.

Oswald Chambers commented on the "Sermon on the Mount" in My Utmost for His Highest, The Door to the Kingdom, saying, "The Sermon on the Mount must produce despair in the natural man; and that is the very thing Jesus means it to do, because immediately we get to despair we are willing to come to Jesus as paupers and to receive from Him. "Blessed are the poor in spirit" that is the first principle of the Kingdom. So long as we have a conceited, self-righteous notion that we can do the thing if God will help us, God has to allow us to go on until we break the neck of our ignorance over some obstacle, then we are willing to come and receive from Him."

The promise of the Kingdom is for those who are poor and humble and recognize their need for the Lord. Theirs is the Kingdom of God. You can know that you're going to heaven right now. You can have access to what the Lord has now if you are poor in spirit. The Kingdom of God and the Kingdom of Heaven are synonymous terms. The broad understanding of the Kingdom of God is the rule of the eternal, sovereign God over the entire universe. He is the king over everything! A narrower understanding of the Kingdom of God is the spiritual rule over those whose hearts and lives have willingly submitted to the King's authority. Jesus said His Kingdom is not of this world. His Kingdom is eternal. Those who do not submit to His authority and reject Christ become part of another kingdom. The kingdom of this world.

Jesus encouraged His disciples to pray for the kingdom of God, emphasizing its importance. He said to them, "When you pray, say:

Our Father in heaven, Hallowed be Your name. Your kingdom come. Your will be done On earth as it is in heaven" (Luke 11:2). According to Acts, before Jesus ascended back to Heaven, the disciples asked Him about the kingdom. He told them of the power that would enable them to proclaim His kingdom to the world. "But you shall receive power when the Holy Spirit has come upon you; and you shall be witnesses to Me in Jerusalem, and in all Judea and Samaria, and to the end of the earth" (Acts 1:8).

The Kingdom of God is real, and it is coming! And the Bible tells us that we who believe are going to be a part of that. When we embrace the proper attitude concerning our poverty of spirit, all of God's blessings become real. Knowing that apart from the Lord, we can do nothing about spiritual poverty releases us to depend on the Lord to provide spiritual wealth. A proper perspective about spiritual poverty leads to a proper attitude concerning sin.

THE SECOND BEATITUDE: THOSE WHO MOURN
Blessed are those who mourn, for they shall be comforted.

This seems like a paradox. How can we be blessed by mourning? It's when we mourn over the sinfulness of sin and the realization that it was our sins that put Christ on the cross! A revelation that sin brings about death and separation from the Father. To mourn over sin is to view sin through God's eyes, interpreting and treating sin the way God does. If someone seeks to cover their sin rather than mourn over it in repentance, they have the wrong attitude toward sin, but the Bible says, "The sacrifices of God are a broken spirit and a contrite heart— these, O God, You will not despise" (Psalm 51:17).

When we truly understand the love of God in that He loved us enough to die for us, and that we have spent a good portion of our lives turning our back on His love and grace, we mourn. The blessing that follows our brokenness is the ultimate comfort of God in the form of eternal salvation. At this point, we realize that despite our rejection of

God, He still loves us. Romans 8:1 tells us: "There is therefore now no condemnation to those who are in Christ Jesus, who do not walk according to the flesh, but according to the Spirit."

We experience the comfort of the Holy Spirit when we ask for forgiveness and mourn over our sins. The Lord shows up and wraps us in His love. His comfort overwhelms us as we mourn, and the Holy Spirit refreshes us. Paul wrote in 2 Corinthians 1:3-5 (ESV): "Blessed be the God and Father of our Lord Jesus Christ, the Father of mercies and God of all comfort, who comforts us in all our affliction, that we may be able to comfort those who are in any affliction, with the comfort with which we ourselves are comforted by God. For as we share abundantly in Christ's sufferings, so through Christ we share abundantly in comfort too."

THE THIRD BEATITUDE: MEEKNESS
Blessed are the the meek, for they shall inherit the earth.

The poverty of spirit leads to mourning over our own sinful condition, which leads to the comfort of the Holy Spirit, and in turn, is followed by meekness. Meekness does not imply weakness or one easily bullied. Meekness in this context means strength under control. Jesus is the ultimate example of meekness. Jesus was God Incarnate come to earth in human form, yet He lived under the confines of humanness. Jesus said, "I am meek and lowly; learn of me." This can be applied to the Christian who is aware of their sinful nature and no longer walks in self-pride but in humility. One of the marks of a true believer is that sense of humility and meekness that says they don't know everything before a Holy God who is all-knowing.

Meekness shows a willingness to submit to and work under the proper authority. It shows a willingness to allow the Spirit of God to work in our lives. What is the promise to those who are meek? The Bible says the meek shall inherit the earth. We can only be meek because we are confident that God watches out for us and He will protect our cause. He will not allow us to end up on the short end of the stick. In the Gospel of Matthew: Expository Thoughts on the Gospels, J. C. Ryle wrote: "Those who are meek are willing to put up with little honor here below, they can bear injuries without resentment, they are not ready to take offense. They are never losers in the long run. One day they will reign upon the earth."

Next, we see the proper perspective concerning the Lord and a desire for more of Him.

THE FOURTH BEATITUDE: FILLED WITH RIGHTEOUSNESS
*Blessed are those who hunger and thirst for righteousness,
for they shall be filled.*

When studying the Beatitudes, we realize they are connected to one another like a chain leading from the first to the last. Once we discover our poverty of spirit, we move on to mourn over our separation from God, which brings about an attitude of meekness, which leads us to a hunger and thirst for righteousness that we might be filled. We now want more of Jesus and more of God's Word!

Referring to Deuteronomy 8:3, Jesus said, "It is written, 'Man shall not live by bread alone, but by every word that proceeds from the mouth of God'" (Matthew 4:4). Jesus is the bread of life and as Christians, we develop an insatiable desire for more of Him because this is how we become spiritually filled.

The psalmist wrote, "As the deer pants for the water brooks, so pants my soul for You, O God," (Psalm 42:1), and, "O God, You are my God; Early will I seek You; my soul thirsts for You; my flesh longs for You in a dry and thirsty land where there is no water. So I have looked for You in the sanctuary, to see Your power and Your glory" (Psalm 63:1-2). Also, "For He satisfies the longing soul, and fills the hungry soul with goodness" (Psalm 107:9).

Do you have a hunger for the Lord? A thirst that seeks to be quenched in Him? Or do you only feed upon those things that hinder your hunger for Christ? If you hunger and thirst for more of Jesus, you will be filled. That is His blessing and promise.

THE FIFTH BEATITUDE: THE MERCIFUL
Blessed are the merciful, for they shall obtain mercy.

When we have the proper perspective about sin that results in repentance and meekness, a desire to be filled with the Lord follows, which leads to a right attitude toward others. One of the attributes of God in Scripture is that He is merciful. Paul tells us in Ephesians 2:4-7 that God is rich in mercy, and in Lamentations, we are told we serve a merciful God who doesn't give us what we deserve: "Through the Lord's mercies, we are not consumed, because His compassions fail not. They are new every morning" (Lamentations 3:22-23).

We can wake up each morning with fresh mercy! And when we realize that He has been merciful to us, we, in turn, show mercy to others. If you desire mercy, you should show mercy, because the same measure that we use toward others will be measured back to us. Jesus told a parable about a ruler who forgave a servant's debts by showing him mercy, but there was an ironic twist to the story when it came time for the servant to forgive another (Matthew 18:22-35).

The Lord likened this parable to those who don't show mercy. How merciful has God been with you? He has forgiven the greatest debt of all that we can never pay back—the bloodshed by Christ on the cross for our eternal salvation. How, then, can we see somebody else who has wronged us and not show mercy to them? Because the Lord has been so merciful toward us, we should ask Him in prayer for help to be merciful to others no matter what they have done or said. In Matthew 9:13, Jesus said, "Go and learn what this means; I desire mercy and not sacrifice." And James wrote, "For judgment is without mercy to the one who has shown no mercy. Mercy triumphs over judgment" (James 2:13).

THE SIXTH BEATITUDE: PURITY OF HEART
Blessed are the pure in heart, for they shall see God.

The Greek word here for the heart is *cardia*, which can be applied to the physical heart within a body but also refers to the spiritual center of one's life, where the thoughts and desires, sense of purpose, the will, understanding and character reside. So, to be pure in heart means to be blameless in who we actually are. Pure in heart means clean, blameless, unstained from guilt. Interestingly the word can refer specifically to that which is purified by fire, or that which is purified through the pruning process. In the ancient Greek, the phrase "pure of heart" has the idea of straightness, honesty, and clarity, and describes someone who isn't constantly dirty from all the little stains that come from contact with the world. A desire exists for purity of heart in the inward man. In the inward life, we want to be pure. Remember the cry of the psalmist's heart, "Create in me a clean heart, O God, and renew a right spirit within me" (Psalm 51:10). God, let the inner person of who I am be pure. To have purity of heart is also to be completely sincere whether in private or public, transparent before God and men.

One of the indictments Jesus brought against the religious leaders, the Pharisees, was their lack of purity internally. Jesus said: "You blind Pharisee! First clean the inside of the cup and the plate, that the outside also may be clean. Woe to you, scribes and Pharisees, hypocrites! For you are like whitewashed tombs, which outwardly appear beautiful, but within are full of dead people's bones and all uncleanness. So you also outwardly appear righteous to others, but within you are full of hypocrisy and lawlessness" (Matthew 23:26-28 ESV).

Jesus told the religious leaders external purity gives the appearance of walking with a pure heart but in truth, their hearts were dead inside. The blessing attached to seeking purity of life unspotted from the world is that they shall see God. The pure in heart shall see things they would not normally see because they are walking with the Lord. Conversely, when we live a life engaged in impure things, this hinders our ability to have a clear vision of the Lord. If there's a secret vice we continually go back to and refer to and engage in, the work of the Spirit within our lives will be hindered. Steering clear of those things that cause impurity greatly impacts our lives.

Concerning the eye-gate, Jesus warned that what goes into the eye affects the mind, which in turn affects the heart (who we are), and then makes its way into our actions. Those who entertain the impurities of life cause their minds to warp; such things as concepts of what healthy relationships look like, God's will, etc., makes its way down into the heart and out into how we live, resulting in an unguarded heart. The Bible says to guard our hearts with all diligence because out of our hearts spring all the issues of life. Jesus tells us we need to be on guard because we live in an impure world. impure, using, for example, innuendos. It is a battle to stay pure in an impure world. In such a desensitized world, including the infiltration of worldly acceptance and ways into the church, some ask themselves if it's even possible to stay pure. And worse, they ask if anyone really cares and conclude that it must not be that big of a deal. But it is possible to live a pure life within an impure world.

A great example of this is Daniel. He was taken against his will to Babylon, a place where people had access to things (the impure things of the world) they never dreamed existed. Here Daniel was all alone as a young man in the prime of his teen years with access to whatever he desired. Every opportunity awaited him under a king who laid out all the delicacies the world had to offer. In other words, whatever a young man would crave was his for the taking. But the amazing thing about Daniel, the Bible tells us, is that before he even got there, he had already purposed in his heart he was not going to defile himself with those things. Long before he got there it was already decided.

As we follow the story of Daniel's life through the Book of Daniel, we see that what kept him pure was his relationship with God. Daniel lived a pure life, undefiled, and that opened him up to see the things that God had for him. Aside from seeing God in heaven one day, we also have the blessing of seeing God work in our lives here and now. God wants to work in our lives to minister to others. We want to be pure vessels God can use for His glory.

Like Daniel, the Apostle Paul mentions the discipline developed in his life. In fact, he said that in his own life he disciplined his body and brought it into submission, lest he would be disqualified from ministering (1 Corinthians 9:27). Paul saw his life in the athletic context within the spiritual sense. In essence, he was saying he had to be like the fine-tuned athlete and could not afford to give in or be distracted because it would disqualify his ability to serve. And though he would not lose his salvation, he could lose the opportunity. He was not willing to do that, so he decided to discipline his body by staying in the Word and prayer to ensure that nothing would come into his life to defile or hinder him from his full potential to be used for the glory of God.

How does one become pure? How is that even possible? It is possible through the Word of God. The Word of God is like detergent to a stain. The Word cleanses and purifies us. The Bible talks about the washing of water through the Word and how God washes our hearts and minds to equip us to remain pure in an impure environment. We live in an impure society. Statistics show that impurity is a huge epidemic even within the church. Impurity is accessible with a click of a button. A person no longer needs to go to a liquor store to purchase a magazine of this nature, running out of the store so nobody sees them. There is a need for purity. If anyone is in bondage to pornography, there is a cure. It begins with repentance and turning to God for the power to overcome.

THE SEVENTH BEATITUDE: PEACEMAKERS
Blessed are the peacemakers,
for they shall be called the sons of God.

Peacemakers, only used one other time in the New Testament (Colossians 1) in reference to peace that comes from the blood of Jesus Christ, has its origins in those who seek to be like Jesus. Paul, when writing to the Romans, said, "If possible, so far as it depends on you, live peaceably with all. Beloved, never avenge yourselves, but leave it to the wrath of God, for it is written, 'Vengeance is mine, I will repay, says the Lord'" (Romans 12:18-19 ESV).

The psalmist declares: "What man is there who desires life and loves many days, that he may see good? Keep your tongue from evil and your lips from speaking deceit. Turn away from evil and do good; seek peace and pursue it" (Psalm 34:12-14 ESV). Are we seeking and pursuing peace? Paul said, "Become complete. Be of good comfort, be of one mind, live in peace; and the God of love and peace will be with you" (2 Corinthians 13:11).

How important it is to seek to be a peacemaker. It is not always possible to be at peace. Suppose you have worked toward peace but are still at odds with a person? As much as it depends upon you, be at peace. If you're a peacemaker, it shows that you are a child of God.

THE EIGHTH BEATITUDE: PERSECUTION
Blessed are those who are persecuted for righteousness sake,
for theirs is the Kingdom of Heaven.

Please note, if we suffer persecution for righteousness' sake, we will be blessed. Jesus said, "Blessed are you when they revile and persecute you, and say all kinds of evil against you falsely for My sake." Notice what Jesus says next. "Rejoice and be exceedingly glad, for great is your reward in heaven, for so they persecuted the prophets who were before you."

The Bible warns us to beware when all men speak well of us. This could be an indication of your Christianity. Not everyone is going to speak well of you if you are living your life for Christ. What should our response be to the world if they speak evil about us? Should we fight back? Should we get into a social media battle with them? Should we block them from everything in our lives? Should we get mad or get even? The response is the opposite of what would be expected of us. Jesus tells us to rejoice! But how is something so unnatural possible? We must focus on what Jesus said about receiving the reward in heaven. We are part of the fraternity of prophets. How can we know that we can choose happiness in the midst of persecution? Because, like the prophets, we know that there is a reward waiting for us in heaven.

In writing to the Romans, Paul, who suffered greatly for the gospel, said, "For I consider that the sufferings of this present time are not worthy to be compared with the glory which shall be revealed in us" (Romans 8:18). There is no comparison to the undefiled glory that awaits us in heaven. We can also rejoice because we can identify with others who have gone before us. But mostly we can identify with Jesus, who suffered wrongfully. Paul wrote to the Philippians that he wanted to know the power of Christ and His resurrection; and, the fellowship of his suffering, being conformed to his death.

In the Book of Acts, after Jesus had ascended to heaven and the Holy Spirit had descended upon the early church, believers began to evangelize locally in Jerusalem. After they were evangelizing, they were brought before the Sanhedrin and warned to stop talking about Jesus, His crucifixion and resurrection. Their response was they could not stop proclaiming the Good News. They could not stop preaching about the things they had seen and heard; they were at an impasse.

The believers kept sharing the gospel and according to Acts, were brought a second time before the Sanhedrin, who did not know what to do to stop the Gospel and its overwhelming evidence of power that was changing lives. Then Gamaliel, one of the Pharisees, posed that if what the apostles were doing was of God, then they wouldn't want to fight against it because they would then be fighting against God. But if it's of man then it will come to nothing. "And when they had called in the apostles, they beat them and charged them not to speak in the name of Jesus, and let them go. Then they left the presence of the council, rejoicing that they were counted worthy to suffer dishonor for the name. And every day, in the temple and from house to house, they did not cease teaching and preaching that the Christ is Jesus" (Acts 5:40-42 ESV).

Jesus taught His disciples about suffering on the "Sermon on the Mount." He said to rejoice and be exceedingly glad. So, His followers considered it a privilege and an honor to be allowed to suffer for His sake. There is a kind of intimate fellowship in the suffering of Christ and being persecuted for righteousness' sake that causes a Christian to rejoice. We can be thankful to God that we are doing something that is affecting the kingdom of darkness. We can be thankful when our lives are making an impact on others and their lives are changing. The devil is bothered by this and we are hammered by the forces of evil. Before becoming a Christian, we were part of the problem but now we are the solution to rescue people from the fires of hell.

What do we see from these attitudes placed before us by the Lord? For one thing, we can understand that the principles of Christianity differ completely from the principles of living in this world. The Beatitudes are the antithesis of worldly living. The characteristics that the Lord praises and blesses are often those characteristics that are despised and looked down upon as weak and worthless in this world. We also come to realize that sometimes these attributes that are seen in the disciples or followers of Jesus aren't always practiced. Only with the help and by the power of the Holy Spirit can these beatitudes be worked into our lives.

3

SALT AND LIGHT

SALT

> "You are the salt of the earth, but if salt has lost its taste, how shall its saltiness be restored? It is no longer good for anything except to be thrown out and trampled under people's feet" (Matthew 5:13 ESV).

Jesus told His disciples they were the salt of the earth. But why would Jesus compare them to salt? There are a few reasons for such an analogy. For one, salt is a preserving influence, and in those days, when Jesus walked the earth, they did not have the means to preserve things that could quickly decay from bacteria. So, to preserve food, people would use salt. Salt was also a precious commodity and used on the trade market. Also, a soldier would be paid in salt, which is where the phrase "Is he worth his salt?" was originated.

Like salt, the church is called to be a preserving influence over the bacteria of sin that comes into this world. The presence of the church in the world can influence the rottenness that may seep into society. Aside from its preserving influence, salt also has a medicinal purpose. A perfect example of this is a visit to the Dead Sea in Israel because this body of water is full of salt and though it can sting, salt's medicinal qualities can heal wounds. As the salt of the earth, we have that same influence.

Every day, as Christians, we come across people who have been scraped from the cares of this world. There are people spiritually wounded with gaping lacerations from a broken relationship or painful divorce. But we have the opportunity to enter into these situations as a healing influence on people who are hurting all around and scarred from living in this world. Jesus said: "For everyone will be seasoned with fire, and every sacrifice will be seasoned with salt. Salt is good, but if the salt loses its flavor, how will you season it? Have salt in yourselves, and have peace with one another" (Mark 9:49-50).

Salt has a preserving and medicinal influence but also creates thirst. Food seasoned with salt makes one thirsty, but a drink of water quenches that thirst. When our lives are characterized by the Beatitudes, it can create a thirst for the things of God in other people. Hopefully, they see our life and wonder what we have that creates such joy in a joyless situation. The world is like a desert wasteland with myriads of people searching for a way to quench their "spiritual" thirst. The bartender's cocktails cannot satisfy the deepest longings of the soul; nor can relationships or careers extinguish this type of thirst, because whatever the world has to offer always leaves people thirsty for more. As Christians, we can point people away from a mirage toward the direction of Jesus, who is the only One who can quench their spiritual thirst. Do our lives influence others toward a relationship with Jesus Christ?

In John chapter 4, Jesus met a woman at Jacob's well who asked Him where to get the living water, of which He spoke. "Jesus answered and said to her, 'Whoever drinks of this water will thirst again, but whoever drinks of the water that I shall give him will never thirst. But the water that I shall give him will become in him a fountain of water springing up into everlasting life.'"

Before Jesus came along, this woman was drinking from the well of relationships. When she got into a conversation with Jesus, He challenged her to call on her husband, to which she told Jesus she had no husband. But she perceived Jesus as a prophet when Jesus said to her, "You have well said, 'I have no husband,' for you have had five husbands, and the one whom you now have is not your husband; in that, you spoke truly" (John 4:18).

The woman at the well had no idea just how thirsty she was until she came into contact with Jesus. Her encounter with the Lord changed her life forever. Christ in us makes all the difference in the world. Does your life make people thirsty for what you have?

Salt also brings flavor to those things that are bland. For some people, life is dull, but those who have salt within themselves bring a sense of seasoning to the table. Christ gives us a reason to rejoice. As believers, He changes our perspective and our lives and draws people to Jesus. However, Jesus warns us with a question: "If the salt loses its flavor, how shall it be seasoned?" (Matthew 5:13).

If the church of Jesus Christ loses its saltiness, its preserving, healing, thirst-creating, life-enhancing influence, what purpose does the church have? If the church loses its salt and fails to be what God called it to be, no longer making an impact, the church becomes a social club that gathers only to meet nice people because it's nice to be nice. Then, what's the point? There is more to the church than the social aspect. However, in some places, that is all there is—a cool vibe. And if there is no substance to a church gathering, and no one is creating a desire for more of Jesus, then something is wrong. Sadly, there has been a decline in America with respect to the saltiness in the church. And if we don't have anything to offer the world, then people will not be able to quench their "spiritual" thirst.

The Book of Acts is a model for us to follow. Its simplicity was effective. First and foremost, the early disciples kept themselves in the Apostle's Doctrine (Word of God), which is crucial to the survival of the church. They continued in worship, fellowship, and prayer — a praying church devoted to the Word, unity, and praises to God. And the church multiplied. He blessed them because the church was salt and light.

The church loses its savor when it compromises the truth of the Word of God or becomes like the world to try to win the world. The congregation can become known for its carnality and divisiveness, and this ruins the influence of the church within the world. As a pastor, I turn the Word back on myself and ask the Lord to examine my heart. Lord, does my life have that sense of salt within my heart? Lord, has the savor begun to dwindle? The only remedy is to get back in the Word, in fellowship and in walking with Jesus. When a Christian walks with Jesus, they become like Him. We are not only called to be the salt of the earth but also to be the light of the world. As we spend time with Jesus, we get to know His heart and His mindset about people who are hurting and lost.

LIGHT

"You are the light of the world. A city set on a hill cannot be hidden. Nor do people light a lamp and put it under a basket, but on a stand, and it gives light to all in the house. In the same way, let your light shine before others, so that they may see your good works and give glory to your Father who is in heaven" (Matthew 5:14-16 ESV).

Jesus compared us to light. If we are followers of Jesus, we identify with the One who is the light of the world. Jesus said: "I am the light of the world. He who follows Me shall not walk in darkness, but have the light of life" (John 8:12). The Bible tells us, "For you were once darkness, but now you are light in the Lord. Walk as children of light" (Ephesians 5:8), and, "You are all sons of light and sons of the day. We are not of the night nor of darkness" (1 Thessalonians 5:5). In Philippians 2:15, we are told why: "… that you may become blameless and harmless, children of God without fault in the midst of a crooked and perverse generation, among whom you shine as lights in the world."

John tells of John the Baptist, who was sent as a light to bear witness of the true light "that all through him might believe" (John 1:7). As Christians, we reflect the light of the Son of God to this dark world. Light was the first thing that God called into existence (Genesis 1:3-5). The sole purpose of light is to shine in darkness in the same way the sole purpose of the believer is to shine in the midst of the darkness that surrounds us. To shine for Christ. Light gives direction. When it's dark, we turn on a light to get a sense of where we are. People in this world are lost in darkness and don't know which way to turn, but when we step in and point them to the ultimate light, Christ, then they can find direction for their lives. As the psalmist says, "Thy word is a lamp unto my feet, and a light unto my path" (Psalm 119:105).

The Bible tells us, "But you are a chosen generation, a royal priesthood, a holy nation, His own special people, that you may proclaim the praises of Him who called you out of darkness into His marvelous light" (1 Peter 2:9). And with this guidance, we can give direction to others like a lighthouse that directs a ship in darkness and a storm. The captain of a ship lost in dark waters sees the beaming light and can steer toward a safe harbor. People outside of Christ are like a ship lost at sea, tossed to and fro. They desire a safe harbor and rest from the storm. As a beacon of the Lord's light, we can direct lost people to the Lord's safe harbor.

Light also brings life. Without light, living things on the earth are not able to survive. Light from the sun provides energy for life on earth. All living organisms on the planet depend directly or indirectly on the light. People in the world are dying because of darkness, which leads to eternal darkness and death. Paul wrote to the Corinthians, "And even if our gospel is veiled, it is veiled to those who are perishing. In their case the god of this world has blinded the minds of the unbelievers, to keep them from seeing the light of the gospel of the glory of Christ, who is the image of God" (2 Corinthians 4:3-4 ESV).

As Christians, we have the message of the light of the Gospel that exposes darkness and gives direction that brings life. Jesus said: "And this is the judgment: the light has come into the world, and people loved the darkness rather than the light because their works were evil. For everyone who does wicked things hates the light and does not come to the light, lest his works should be exposed. But whoever does what is true comes to the light, so that it may be clearly seen that his works have been carried out in God" (John 3:19-21 ESV).

When we hide in darkness, our eyes can become accustomed to the dark; however, once someone turns on the light our hiding place is exposed. When we shine the light of Christ into a dark world, people might run from the potential influence of our testimony. Some may shun us because the light of Jesus brings conviction. Have you ever noticed that in places such as bars it is always dark? People don't want to be seen. Are you in the shadows of darkness? "But if we walk in the light as He is in the light, we have fellowship with one another, and the blood of Jesus Christ His Son cleanses us from all sin" (1 John 1:7).

Light exposes darkness, and the light of God's Word has a way of exposing darkness within the heart. Likewise, light cheers the heart like a sunny day after gloomy weather. When the sun appears through the clouds after several days of rainy weather, we can compare this to the joy of the Lord shining into our hearts than were once clouded with "foul weather."

In conclusion, light cannot be hidden. Jesus likened a church to a city that when set upon a hill could not be hidden. The church isn't designed to blend in with the world. Some believers use a dimmer and travel incognito with their Christian walk rather than shine bright for the Lord. But we wouldn't turn on a lamp to hide it under a table. The lamp's purpose is to illuminate the darkness just as the purpose of a Christian is to shed light on Jesus as the way, truth, and life that no man can come to the Father except through Him.

We are to shine in such a way that men may see our good works and glorify our Father in heaven. The moon is the light that shines in the darkness. But the moon receives light from the sun. The sun shines upon the moon to light up the night. We reflect the light of the Son of God to light up the darkness that is in the world. In times past, oil was used to light a lamp. Oil is symbolic of the Holy Spirit. When our "light" dims, we can ask the Lord to fill us with the Holy Spirit that we may burn brightly once again. "This is the message we have heard from him and proclaim to you, that God is light, and in him is no darkness at all. If we say we have fellowship with him while we walk in darkness, we lie and do not practice the truth. But if we walk in the light, as he is in the light, we have fellowship with one another, and the blood of Jesus his Son cleanses us from all sin" (1 John 1:5-7 ESV).

We are salt and light. Let us not lose our flavor and witness. If we live for Christ, God can use us for His glory. As the moon is the light that shines in the night, reflecting the light of the sun, let us reflect the light of Christ to the world.

4

JESUS FULFILLS THE LAW

Jesus said, "Do not think that I have come to abolish the Law or the Prophets; I have not come to abolish them but to fulfill them. For truly, I say to you, until heaven and earth pass away, not an iota, not a dot, will pass from the Law until all is accomplished. Therefore, whoever relaxes one of the least of these commandments and teaches others to do the same will be called least in the kingdom of heaven, but whoever does them and teaches them will be called great in the kingdom of heaven. For I tell you, unless your righteousness exceeds that of the scribes and Pharisees, you will never enter the kingdom of heaven" (Matthew 5:17-20 ESV).

Jesus opens His "Sermon on the Mount" in third person with the Beatitudes; then, using second person, Jesus compares believers to salt and light. Now, Jesus speaks in first person as the ultimate authority on the Law of God when He declares, "I say to you." As the popularity of Jesus continued to grow, a question swelled in the minds of the people: Is Jesus really the Messiah? They had listened to His sermons and witnessed the miracles He performed. Mark 1:23-28 tells us that after the deliverance of a demon-possessed man, the people stood in amazement!

There was a noticeable difference between the ministry of Jesus versus the ministry of the scribes and Pharisees that was clearly obvious. Jesus spoke with authority and power. His ministry was associated with the broken, hurting, and diseased sinners, and He served the people by reaching out to them. His character was marked by humility, meekness, and love. On the other hand, the scribes and Pharisees were marked by religious pride, intolerance, and prejudice.

Another question on the minds of the common people, and especially the religious leaders, circled around how Jesus felt about the Law. The scribes and Pharisees spent their lives studying the Law. They knew no one could fulfill God's Law perfectly so they developed traditions to accompany the Law. But these traditions were extremely difficult to follow and humanly impossible. These manmade traditions added to the Law nurtured an attitude of self-righteousness and cultivated a life of hypocrisy. These traditions became so ingrained in the religious life that people elevated tradition above the Word of God. The keeping of the traditions became the real standard of righteousness according to the religious leaders.

Therefore, Jesus presented God's standard of righteousness for the religious leaders to consider. God's standard goes far beyond the external and into the heart of the matter. In essence, the Bible explains Christ's relationship to the Law: "Do not think that I have come to abolish the Law or the Prophets; I have not come to abolish them but to fulfill them. For truly, I say to you, until heaven and earth pass away, not an iota, not a dot, will pass from the Law until all is accomplished" (Matthew 5:17-18 ESV). And the Christian's relationship to the law is mapped out: "Therefore whoever relaxes one of the least of these commandments and teaches others to do the same will be called least in the kingdom of heaven, but whoever does them and teaches them will be called great in the kingdom of heaven. For I tell you, unless your righteousness exceeds that of the scribes and Pharisees, you will never enter the kingdom of heaven" (Matthew 5:19-20 ESV).

When Jesus states the negative, there's an implication that this was one thought circulating and propagated by the religious leaders. They believed Jesus was doing away with the Laws of Moses, teaching doctrine contrary to the Law. But Jesus was not violating the Law. Instead, His ministry violated the traditions of men.

In the Gospel record, one of their traditions addressed hygiene and detailed the proper and acceptable way of washing hands before eating. The water had to be measured out, and the hands had to be placed into the basin in a particular manner, mindful not to touch certain boundaries set by the religious leaders. And if a person did not wash their hands according to their specifications and consumed food, they were deemed unclean and sinful. Jesus resisted this practice. What goes into a person does not defile, but that which comes out of a person does defile.

The religious leaders also challenged Jesus about fasting. Why didn't the disciples fast twice a week like them? Why wasn't this religious practice followed by Jesus? Their fasting was to get the attention of God to get Him to grant their wishes. They expected God to fulfill an obligation, which was a huge misunderstanding of the very purpose of fasting. Too, the leaders fasted in public view to prove to the people that they were religious. But this practice was connected to their traditions and not to the Law of God.

These traditions became increasingly more absurd, especially as it related to the Sabbath Day. Once, the disciples of Jesus walked through a field on the Sabbath, picking heads of grain to chew on their way. But when the Pharisees saw it, they accused them of harvesting on the Sabbath Day, a violation of their manmade tradition, not a violation of the Law of God. There were so many prohibitions placed on the Sabbath Day, a day designated by God for rest, that the Sabbath Day became more a day of work than rest.

The Bible says on the Sabbath day, you are not able to bear a burden. The religious leaders decided to define "burden." They determined that food equal to the weight of a fig constituted a burden. Therefore, if a person picked up a fig, they just carried a burden! Anything more than a swallow of milk would be considered a burden. Honey applied to anything that exceeded a small wound for medicinal purposes was labeled as work. Water to moisten as an eye salve was acceptable, as was ink to write no more than two letters of the alphabet. Anything beyond these established restrictions was considered a burden.

The even stricter interpretations defined as "labor" included using a crutch, prosthetic limbs, false teeth, picking up a child, and administration of medical treatment short of life-threatening. Jesus was continually throwing over these traditions that frustrated people on the Sabbath. Such as the multiple times Jesus performed miracles on purpose on the Sabbath. The "religion" of the religious leaders was reduced to external observance. They drew near to God with their lips and outward rituals, but in reality, their hearts were far from God. For this reason, Jesus performed miracles on the Sabbath day. He wanted to reveal the authentic interpretation of God's Word to the people and put to rest any misconceptions about His relationship to the Law of God.

There was the man with a withered hand He healed at the synagogue on a Sabbath. It's interesting to note that the religious leaders knew the heart of Jesus and that they knew He would be drawn to heal this man on the Sabbath. They knew if anyone had an issue in that synagogue, Jesus would find them to meet their needs. But Jesus already knew this was a setup. So, he proceeded (Mark 3:1-6). On another occasion, it was on the Sabbath that Jesus went to the Pool of Bethesda where He asked a paralytic man if he would like to be healed (John 5:2-17).

THE LAW AND THE PROPHETS

The Law and the Prophets was a classification that referred to all of the Old Testament scripture. The Greek word *kataluo* means to overthrow. In ancient Greek, to overthrow meant to invalidate institutions and laws connected to the governing forces. The religious leaders accused Jesus of invalidating the law and seeking to replace the law, but in reality, He was not adhering to the traditions of men that were attached to the law. The irony of the accusations by these men that Jesus was breaking the law is that these men were actually in violation of breaking God's laws. Jesus said, "I came to fulfill the law."

Considering the law Jesus came to fulfill, the Jews looked at this law in a few ways. First, the Ten Commandments were given by God to Moses to give to the nation of Israel. Then, there is the Pentateuch (the first five books of the Old Testament) written by Moses, followed by all the books of the Old Testament. But the problem with religious leaders of the day was their allegiance to rabbinical traditions and that they equated these traditions as equal to God's law.

The Pharisees believed that the law saved men, was the summary of all wisdom and represented everything to the Jew, including the keeping of the law to secure a good relationship with God. But the law required death for disobedience. A person who did not keep the whole law was considered guilty of the whole law. If someone had offended in any point, they were deemed guilty of the whole law and under the curse of the law, which is why a sacrificial system was established. In this way, people could atone for their sins. The New Testament explains the real purpose of the law, which was given to reveal how unrighteous we are and how incapable we are of keeping the law, and the Apostle Paul mentions this.

> "But the Scripture imprisoned everything under sin, so that the promise by faith in Jesus Christ might be given to those who believe. Now before faith came, we were held captive under the law, imprisoned until the coming faith would be revealed. So then, the law was our guardian until Christ came, in order that we might be justified by faith. But now that faith has come, we are no longer under a guardian" (Galatians 3:22-25 ESV).

If the law wasn't given to make us righteous, then what was its purpose? The law reveals that we are unrighteous sinners. People who say they live by the Ten Commandments do not understand what that means because no one, except Jesus, can keep these moral laws perfectly. When we look to pattern our lives according to God's law, we fall short. Everyone has broken God's commandments. However, when we see that we are unable to produce the sacrifices that keep us pure on our own, the law drives us to Christ so we can be justified by faith.

Jesus came to fulfill the law, which was moral, judicial, and ceremonial. Morally speaking, Jesus fulfilled the Law of God because He was without sin. "For He made Him who knew no sin to be sin for us, that we might become the righteousness of God in Him" (2 Corinthians 5:21). He was the lamb without spot or blemish and became the ultimate sacrifice for our sins.

Also, Jesus is the fulfillment of every single one of God's laws and prophecies in the Old Testament, which portrays a foreshadowing of Jesus Christ and points to Him as the fulfillment of the law. The writer of Hebrews clarifies that animal sacrifices were insufficient. "For the law, having a shadow of the good things to come, and not the very image of the things, can never with these same sacrifices, which they offer continually year by year, make those who approach perfect" (Hebrews 10:1).

Jesus fulfilled the law and the prophecies and He validates the authority of God's Word: "For assuredly, I say to you, till heaven and earth pass away, one jot or one tittle will by no means pass from the law till all is fulfilled" (Matthew 5:18). In other words, not the least stroke of a pen; the word jot in Hebrew (yodh) refers to the smallest letter in that alphabet, which is equivalent to a comma. Jesus was saying that all of God's Word was going to be fulfilled, even something one would classify as insignificant as a comma!

The law was fulfilled perfectly through the life and death of Jesus.

The law required and demanded a payment for sin. Jesus fulfilled the law and paid for the sins of the world by shedding His own blood on our behalf. As believers, what is our relationship to the law? The Bible tells us: "Therefore, whoever relaxes one of the least of these commandments and teaches others to do the same will be called least in the kingdom of heaven, but whoever does them and teaches them will be called great in the kingdom of heaven. For I tell you, unless your righteousness exceeds that of the scribes and Pharisees, you will never enter the kingdom of heaven" (Matthew 5:19-20 ESV).

In these verses, Jesus is calling out the religious leaders of the day. Though teachers of the law, these men also violated the law, living contrary to their teachings. These leaders instructed people to live by their manmade traditions but then created loopholes for themselves and thus were living in hypocrisy. Due to their misinterpretations of the law as well as their added traditions, these religious leaders were annulling the law, making God's Word of no effect in the lives of the people. The Pharisees made a big deal out of small things and a little deal out of huge things. Jesus rebuked their sinful behavior. "Woe to you, scribes and Pharisees, hypocrites! For you pay tithe of mint and anise and cumin and have neglected the weightier matters of the law: justice and mercy and faith. These you ought to have done, without leaving the others undone" (Matthew 23:23).

The Pharisees were meticulous in little things yet neglectful of the weightier matters of the law. For instance, as part of their religious tithing practice, they would pour spices across a table and divvy up a portion of the tiny granules to equal a tenth of the whole to God. But they were void of love, mercy, and compassion toward people. God is far more concerned about the weightier matters than if He got enough spices! Sadly, some people live their lives more concerned about petty little things and neglect more important things. Jesus makes it emphatically clear that this is no way to live. The Pharisees interpreted the law on a strictly physical sense when, in reality, it went beyond the outward to the inward. Hypocrisy is a great detriment to the church today and hinders the work of God. While everyone is a hypocrite to some degree, people hold believers to a certain standard. God forbid that we live a hypocritical life.

The Pharisees confused the people who did not speak Hebrew. Many of the common people spoke Chaldean or Aramaic and were dependent on the scribes and Pharisees, their spiritual leaders, for interpretation. However, the religious leaders misinterpreted God's law, which caused a heavy burden on society. The Pharisees created 613 additional regulations to the original "Ten Commandments," an impossible ruling for people to live righteous lives before the Lord. To add to the contriteness, these Pharisees paraded through villages and towns wearing a showpiece called phylacteries (small leather boxes containing Hebrew texts, worn by Jewish men at morning prayer as a reminder to keep the law) that protruded from their foreheads for all to see. As well, they would wrap the words containing the Law of God about their wrists to embody the law literally. "Therefore you shall lay up these words of mine in your heart and in your soul, and bind them as a sign on your hand, and they shall be as frontlets between your eyes" (Deuteronomy 11:18). These men gloried in outward righteousness and Jesus warned the people accordingly. "Therefore whatever they tell you to observe, that observe and do, but do not do according to their works; for they say, and do not do" (Matthew 23:3).

Further, Jesus makes a bold statement concerning the law. "For I say to you, that unless your righteousness exceeds the righteousness of the scribes and Pharisees, you will by no means enter the kingdom of heaven" (Matthew 5:20). Imagine the disciples of Jesus who heard these words for the first time. They didn't know anyone more righteous than the religious leaders.

Through the "Sermon on the Mount," Jesus was mapping out genuine righteous behavior. He began with the Beatitudes when He said a believer is one who is poor in spirit. One who is supposed to mourn over their condition, thirst for righteousness and obtain mercy with a pure heart to live peaceably with all men, rejoicing in persecution for the Lord's sake, and becoming salt and light to bring a dying world to Jesus. Now He was saying that outward righteousness does not make anyone righteous in the sight of God. A believer must clothe themselves with the righteousness of Christ. The only righteousness acceptable to God was righteousness imputed from Christ.

The Bible says our righteousness is as filthy rags. Therefore, activities and rituals at church cannot save us. A seat in the sanctuary does not equal a seat in heaven. Our righteousness is not found in works but in Christ by faith in what He has accomplished. And His righteousness is made available to us by receiving Him through faith. Jesus fulfilled the demands of the law, and He fulfilled the prophetic law, but He also pointed out that we have a relationship to the law. The Bible tells us that the law is good because it converts the soul. And we can live according to God's Word through Jesus as the Bible tells us in Romans. "For those who live according to the flesh set their minds on the things of the flesh, but those who live according to the Spirit, the things of the Spirit" (Romans 8:5).

In another passage, the Bible tells us Jesus fulfilled the law so we could live according to the righteous requirement of God. "For Christ is the end of the law for righteousness to everyone who believes" (Romans 10:4). God's righteousness through faith is further explained in Romans 3:21-26.

Faith in Christ is the fulfillment of the law, and we are clothed in His righteousness. "And you, being dead in your trespasses and the uncircumcision of your flesh, He has made alive together with Him, having forgiven you all trespasses, having wiped out the handwriting of requirements that was against us, which was contrary to us. And He has taken it out of the way, having nailed it to the cross" (Colossians 2:13-14). Therefore, Christ redeems us from the law that condemns us, and there is a contrast between what the religious leaders were teaching and what Jesus taught. As the ultimate authority, Jesus continues His sermon and begins to explain the real intention of the law for the disciples to understand their relationship to the law.

5

THE ROOT OF THE PROBLEM: ANGER!

"You have heard that it was said to those of old, 'You shall not murder; and whoever murders will be liable to judgment." (Matthew 5:21 ESV).

We are to live according to the Old Testament commandment of the Lord found in Exodus 20:13, which says, "You shall not murder." In the "Sermon on the Mount," Jesus takes this a step further to the root of the problem, which is anger. "But I say to you that everyone who is angry with his brother will be liable to judgment; whoever insults his brother will be liable to the council; and whoever says, 'You fool!' will be liable to the hell of fire" (Matthew 5:22 ESV).

Anger stems from the heart. Though the Pharisees professed that they followed the Ten Commandments, Jesus shone a light into their hearts where such a violation of the Law is activated. A person commits murder because the idea is already in their heart to carry out the action. Cain killed his brother Abel out of anger because God accepted Abel's sacrifice and rejected Cain's sacrifice (Genesis 4:4-8).

The Pharisees had purposed in their hearts to crucify Jesus, but Jesus was already aware of their hidden agenda. He said, "You are of your father, the devil, and the desires of your father you want to do. He was a murderer from the beginning and does not stand in the truth, because there is no truth in him. When he speaks a lie, he speaks from his own resources, for he is a liar and the father of it" (John 8:44).

The Bible says, "Whoever hates his brother is a murderer, and you know that no murderer has eternal life abiding in him" (1 John 3:15). Though undetected outwardly hatred can take root inside the heart of a person and turn into bitterness. Eventually, anger that escalates into hatred is carried from the inside out, and some people express this deep anger with hurtful, thoughtless words or violent actions. Jesus tells us, "For out of the abundance of the heart the mouth speaks" (Matthew 12:34).

Anger stored in the heart eventually comes out. The tongue is a spark and sets the forest of unresolved issues on fire. Ephesians instructs us about anger: "Be angry, and do not sin: do not let the sun go down on your wrath, nor give place to the devil" (Ephesians 4:26-27). Of course, this can be easier said than done, but it is wise to consider what Jesus had to say about storing anger and how malice can affect our lives: "Come to terms quickly with your accuser while you are going with him to court, lest your accuser hand you over to the judge, and the judge to the guard, and you be put in prison" (Matthew 5:25 ESV).

Anger affects our speech, our attitude, and how we think. Anger also affects our worship. It's difficult to lift our hands in worship to the Lord if we are holding a grudge against someone. It's important to get right with the Lord by making things right with others. When we give our frustrations over to the Lord, we can then seek to make amends. God is a God of reconciliation. That's His heart.

As we look at what the Lord has to say about anger and its repercussions, we can ask the Lord to search our hearts and apply His principles for reconciliation. In this exercise, we might ask ourselves if we need to reconcile with anyone in our lives. And if there is someone who did not respond to an olive branch, then we can be comforted by the Word of God instructing us on Christian behavior in these matters. "Therefore, "If your enemy is hungry, feed him; If he is thirsty, give him a drink; For in so doing you will heap coals of fire on his head." Do not be overcome by evil, but overcome evil with good" (Romans 12:24-25).

Moses chose an attitude of humility when the sons of Korah wrongly accused him (Numbers 16:3-5). Then there's Jesus nailed to the cross, dying for the sins of the world, and as He's nailed there, beaten beyond recognition of a man, people spitting in His face, cursing Him, the Bible says, "And the people stood looking on. But even the rulers with them sneered, saying, "He saved others; let Him save Himself if He is the Christ, the chosen of God" (Luke 23:35). Injustice! But what had Jesus just said? "Father, forgive them, for they know not what they do" (Luke 23:24).

When we consider Jesus in this place of total humility, we know that there is so much more the Lord can do to conform us into His image. If Jesus had saved Himself, He would not have been able to save others. Our Lord and Savior hung on a cross to save us and to give us the ability to follow Him and to be like Him toward others. To emulate the Lord, we need the Holy Spirit in our hearts to change us and not allow bitterness to fester and grow, but rather to allow the Lord to remove any roots of bitterness and to plant something beautiful instead.

The tree of bitterness bears rotten fruit, but the fruit of the Spirit grows love, joy, peace, gentleness, and faithfulness, kindness, and self-control. These things blossom when properly planted in our hearts. Yielding to the Lord gives us the ability to prevent anything from hindering us to follow His example with a clean heart.

6

MURDER AND ADULTERY FROM THE HEART

Jesus begins by looking at the sixth commandment of the law: "You have heard that it was said to those of old, 'You shall not murder; and whoever murders will be liable to judgment'" (Matthew 5:21 ESV).

MURDER BEGINS IN THE HEART

He continued to elaborate on the concept of murder as it relates to the heart: "But I say to you that everyone who is angry with his brother will be liable to judgment; whoever insults his brother will be liable to the council; and whoever says, 'You fool!' will be liable to the hell of fire. So if you are offering your gift at the altar and there remember that your brother has something against you, leave your gift there before the altar and go. First be reconciled to your brother, and then come and offer your gift. Come to terms quickly with your accuser while you are going with him to court, lest your accuser hand you over to the judge, and the judge to the guard, and you be put in prison. Truly, I say to you, you will never get out until you have paid the last penny" (Matthew 5:22-26 ESV).

Certainly, the people knew that it was said, "You shall not murder." Moses relayed that in Exodus 20:13. Murder means to kill someone intentionally with premeditation. And those in the presence of Jesus hearing this sermon would be able to say that they had kept the law. But Jesus points out that the Law of God goes deeper than the act of murder itself. Jesus looks at the root cause of murder, which the law condemns, and He clarifies where murder comes from, and that it begins in the heart.

If a person takes the life of another person, the action only proves they were already a murderer within their heart. The Bible says in Proverbs 4:23, "Guard your heart with all diligence for out of it spring the issues of life." Anger unguarded could lead someone to take the life of another person.

In the Old Testament, the story of Cain and Abel exemplifies the truth and how unchecked anger led to murder. Cain's hatred for his brother began in his heart. The resentment over God's acceptance of Abel's sacrifice and rejection of his sacrifice began to grow, and in a moment when only God was looking, Cain took the life of his brother. The Lord held Cain accountable for his brother, saying his blood cried out from the ground! (Genesis 4). Cain suffered the consequences for the murder of Abel, but it all began in his heart.

Hatred and murder are incited by the devil. The Pharisees hated Jesus. He said of the Pharisees that they were of their father, the devil, because the devil was a murderer from the beginning. The Pharisees were envious of Jesus, and they carried out their hatred and anger by nailing Him to a cross at Calvary. Apostle John wrote a strong word in this epistle that revealed a person could be a murderer in their heart: "Whoever hates his brother is a murderer, and you know that no murderer has eternal life abiding in him" (1 John 3:15).

We cannot let hatred and bitterness go unchecked because it leads to more destructive behavior. Sometimes our unbridled anger can be verbalized in harshly spoken words. When this occurs, we have broken

God's law and need to repent. If, however, we allow this to remain, we will be affected in different ways. Harboring hatred has an impact on our time of worship. Jesus said, "If you bring your gift to the altar and there remember that your brother has something against you, leave your gift there before the altar, and go your way. First, be reconciled to your brother and then come and offer your gift."

When you're in the House of the Lord, you want to seek Him but may feel blocked and distracted, unable to enter in, because the seething hatred in your heart for that person has taken over your mind. Not only does hatred hinder worship, but it hinders your witness. The Bible speaks of wisdom concerning anger: "A soft answer turns away wrath, but a harsh word stirs up anger" (Proverbs 15:1 ESV), and, "With patience a ruler may be persuaded, and a soft tongue will break a bone" (Proverbs 25:15 ESV). While it is difficult to imagine that gentle words can break a bone, the Bible says it is possible. When you find yourself tempted to come unglued with anger, stop and pray for the Holy Spirit to give you self control.

ADULTERY STEMS FROM THE HEART

Next, Jesus expounds upon God's law concerning adultery citing the seventh of God's ten commandments: "You have heard that it was said, 'You shall not commit adultery.' But I say to you that everyone who looks at a woman with lustful intent has already committed adultery with her in his heart" (Matthew 5:27 ESV).

Adultery is a sexual relationship outside of marriage, which the Lord condemns within His law. God told Moses: "And you shall not lie sexually with your neighbor's wife and so make yourself unclean with her" (Leviticus 18:20 ESV). The penalty under the Old Testament law then was death for both adulterer and adulteress. "If a man commits adultery with the wife of his neighbor, both the adulterer and the adulteress shall surely be put to death" (Leviticus

20:10 ESV). Deuteronomy 22 discusses in detail the laws of sexual morality and includes reparations for intruding upon a maiden.

The sweet psalmist of Israel and shepherd anointed by God, King David, was referred to as a man after God's own heart. A study of David's life serves to inspire a believer to rise above any circumstance. Whether David was facing the giant Goliath, who menaced the land, defeating him in one single throw of a stone from his slingshot; or, receiving the anointing of God by Samuel to replace Saul, in general, this man led an admirable life. And yet, there is a sad mark on his legacy concerning his sin with Bathsheba, who was a married woman. One decision led to the next decision, which led to the next decision until he fell into sin. After that, David was confronted by his friend, Nathan the prophet (2 Samuel 12:1-6).

Nathan told King David that he was the man in his story. Not only had he taken Bathsheba into his tent, but to cover up her pregnancy from their tryst, he had her husband sent to the front lines. David, the man after God's heart, had committed a tragic sin, and although he deserved to die according to God's law, the Lord had mercy on him. David and Bathsheba's son, Solomon, who wrote so many of the Proverbs, gives an important warning concerning God's Word in the matter of adultery, and how the failure to listen to warnings would lead to dire consequences (Proverbs 6:20-35.)

Growing up in a household that included David's decision to have an adulterous union with a married woman must have influenced Solomon to warn others about the consequences that would follow. God's Word is a lamp for illumination to give us insight and direct our paths. Reproofs of instruction are a way of life to keep us from evil and flattering tongues of seducers. To give in to lust is to be reduced to a crust of bread. And those who participate in such actions destroy their own souls. A very sobering warning that one careless decision can bring your life to nothing. A moment of pleasure can ruin all that is precious and valuable from God. Such a sacrifice can never be regained.

Many who listened to the "Sermon on the Mount" may have felt relieved if they had been married and faithful to the same woman. But then Jesus showed them the intention of the law. Even if someone had not committed the physical act of adultery, they could still be guilty if they lusted in their hearts. From that standpoint, they would have broken God's law. In this sense, Peter warned about the depravity of false teachers (2 Peter 2:12-16).

Adultery begins with wandering eyes, which then makes its way to mind and into the heart and soul of a person. Jesus taught that while it is possible to appear moral and faithful outwardly, adultery and lust can take hold in the privacy of one's heart. Those who break God's law that says, "You shall not commit adultery," began the spiral downward from a look or a conversation that crosses the line. Then, a choice is made whether to entertain those thoughts or to take every thought captive to the obedience of Christ. To let the seed be planted or to uproot it immediately. To run for your life or to sit there. To take the way of escape or to refuse it. No one is above this type of behavior. If the man after God's own heart who slew giants for the nation of Israel could fall, anybody can.

In his epistle, James wrote a warning about temptation. "Let no one say when he is tempted, 'I am tempted by God'; for God cannot be tempted by evil, nor does He Himself tempt anyone. But each one is tempted when he is drawn away by his own desires and enticed. Then, when desire has conceived, it gives birth to sin; and sin, when it is full-grown, brings forth death. Do not be deceived, my beloved brethren" (James 1:13-16). James said what had already been described by Jesus. Temptation begins with a thought, and from within gives way to sin. Sin planted like a seed in one's heart eventually brings forth a kind of harvest crop that comes forth from the ground.

Job said he had made a covenant with his eyes. A covenant was a binding agreement known in the ancient Near East. Job went on to say, "How then could I gaze upon a young woman?" (Job 31:1), meaning (in Hebrew) to carefully consider (rather than a casual glance) when he had already purposed in his heart to keep his gaze in check. The Bible tells us to bring every thought captive to the obedience of Christ (2 Corinthians 10:5). Today, we live in a culture that applauds and promotes lust. But, like Job, a person has to make the decision not to go down that path long in advance. It doesn't work to make such a covenant on the spot! The consequences of giving in to lust must be weighed in advance to decide to avoid temptation. Because temptation will always come knocking at the door.

Before Christ, we may have looked at temptation as an opportunity. But, in Christ, we must die daily to our fleshly desires to reckon our old person dead. On the subject of our human nature, D. L. Moody, later in life, was asked by a young minister, "When did you lose your eye for a young woman?" And his response was, "I'll let you know." What poet Ralph Waldo Emerson wrote is often quoted: "Sow a thought, and you reap an action; sow an action, and you reap a habit; sow a habit, and you reap a character; sow a character, and you reap a destiny." The mathematics involving the consequences of sin is always the same. Sin adds to your sorrow and subtracts from your joy, multiplies your problems, and divides your heart.

Today, the instant access to pornography is a significant factor, and like lethal poison, it affects households of men, women, and children. According to statistics, most elementary school children have access to a smartphone, and some know how to use the device better than their parents. In a matter of seconds, an image can defile them and reel in their minds forever. Data also shows a staggering number of subscribers addicted to pornography within the church. This silent killer absent of accountability is impacting the integrity of families. Those who participate in this vile sin live in bondage.

But Jesus gives us insight on how to overcome a life in bondage to sin. Consider His words: "If your right eye causes you to sin, pluck it out and cast it from you; for it is more profitable for you that one of your members perish than for your whole body to be cast into hell. And if your right hand causes you to sin, cut it off and cast it from you; for it is more profitable for you that one of your members perish than for your whole body to be cast into hell" (Matthew 5:29-30).

The word "to sin" in these verses is translated "to stumble." Translated from the Greek, the word is skandalon, which means a trap, or a snare and a stumbling block; where we get the English derivative "scandalize," to offend in the moral sense, trip up or entice. If a thing causes one to sin and leads them in that direction, then what is the best course of action? According to Jesus' words in this portion of the "Sermon on the Mount," you have to pluck the temptation out and cast it from your life! Jesus is not saying to literally pluck your eyes out because then no one would have any eyes. All of us have sinned with our eyes, our hands, or in some other way. Jesus is saying we must deal drastically with sin. To rationalize temptation is not scriptural because our flesh is at war with our spirit.

Though this behavior is acceptable with society, Jesus says if temptation is leading one to sin, it must be removed from their life. As believers, the Bible makes us aware of certain behaviors and admonishes us on how to conduct our lives. What was acceptable before we received Christ may no longer be acceptable in light of our new life in Christ.

Sin is like a malignant tumor that if not properly excised, can cause death. A surgeon would not leave a little bit of a deadly tumor to fester and metastasize infecting the rest of the body. The Bible tells us that a little leaven leavens the whole lump (Galatians 5:9). It doesn't take a lot of sin to destroy a whole life. If we don't deal drastically with sin and cut it off completely, it will come back and deal drastically with us.

King Saul, in the Old Testament, is a prime example of a man who went from a humble servant of God to despair. The Bible says when the Spirit of God first came upon Saul's life, he became a new man and was given a new heart. Saul became a beautiful picture of the work of

God, prophesying, and living a victorious life. However, as time went on, Saul rebelled against God's plan and compromised his position of authority, disregarding the warnings of God and Samuel, doing things his own way. Eventually, the Bible records, at the end of his life, Saul admitted that he played the fool and erred exceedingly.

When Saul was king, he was unrepentant, prideful and refused to respond to the Lord's instructions to Samuel for him to wipe out everything connected to the Amalekites, a wicked people who had no mercy on the nation of Israel. But when Saul went into battle, he not only spared Agag the king and some of the other Amalekites, but took spoils, the best of livestock, thinking he had done all the Lord asked of him, and he brought Amalekite sheep and oxen as a sacrifice to the Lord. Saul's crown was taken from him that day. Years later, when Saul went into his final battle against the Philistines, he and his sons perished (1 Samuel 31), but it was an Amalekite (2 Samuel 1) who beheaded Saul whose body was then fastened to a wall in Beth Shan. What he didn't deal with earlier came back later to deal with him.

When we hear a story like this, it is time to turn the Word onto ourselves to ask the Lord if there is any leaven in our lives, any root that needs to be removed from impacting our lives and the lives of others. Maybe it's at the office. He's very nice, says nice things to you, compliments you, gave you a gift card to your favorite coffee shop, blah, blah blah. But it's dangerous. Maybe it's through emails, or you connect with an old friend on Facebook, and she still looks great! And so you start going down that road. Before long, you become secretive about this person, and if you don't repent, the whole thing will blow up in your face. "But if you do not do so, then take note, you have sinned against the Lord; and be sure your sin will find you out" (Numbers 32:23).

This type of destructive behavior must be cut off immediately before it can take root. A flirtation is offensive to God. The Bible encourages us to apply, memorize, and ponder God's Word to combat the constant bombardment of temptation for us to give in to our fleshly desires. Paul wrote to the Romans: "Therefore, do not let sin reign in your mortal body, that you should obey it in its lusts. And do not present your members as instruments of unrighteousness to sin, but present yourselves to God as being alive from the dead, and your members as instruments of righteousness to God. For sin shall not have dominion over you, for you are not under law but under grace" (Romans 6:12-14).

We have power over sin. At one time, sin did have dominion over us; we were a slave to sin, and we could not overcome; we were unable to escape, in bondage to sin. But now, in Christ, we have the same power that raised Jesus from the dead dwelling in us, giving us the ability to overcome our flesh, which once was able to subdue us. Grace empowers us and gives us the ability to overcome that which used to bring us into bondage. "Therefore, do not let sin reign in your mortal body."

We are instructed not to present our bodies in an unrighteous manner but to present ourselves to the Lord as an instrument of righteousness. The good news is we have the power to make the right decision. Peter wrote concerning conduct that glorifies God and not the flesh: "Beloved, I beg you as sojourners and pilgrims, abstain from fleshly lusts which war against the soul, having your conduct honorable among the Gentiles, that when they speak against you as evildoers, they may, by your good works, which they observe, glorify God in the day of visitation" (1 Peter 2:11-12). And Paul wrote, "But put on the Lord Jesus Christ, and make no provision for the flesh, to fulfill its lusts" (Romans 13:14).

We control our fleshly desires by "putting on the Lord Jesus Christ," and we don't make provision for the flesh. If we make provision for the flesh, we are going to give in to the flesh. Every time we make provision for our flesh, it will gladly take the provision and will overcome the work of the Spirit in our life.

For example, a person who has a drinking problem would not want to keep a cabinet stocked with liquor, because in a moment of weakness, they could avail themselves of the provision. The person who struggles in the area of pornography and does not have the right amount of accountability to withstand can easily give in to the strong pull of this fleshly desire. In other words, whatever we make provision for, the flesh will respond. The battle between the flesh (the life we once lived governed by our fleshly appetites) and the spirit (our life in Christ) is a daily fight. We are caught between heaven and hell. But the Bible tells us, "No temptation has overtaken you except such as is common to man; but God is faithful, who will not allow you to be tempted beyond what you are able, but with the temptation will also make the way of escape, that you may be able to bear it" (1 Corinthians 10:13).

Jesus gives us a great example of what to do when tempted. Every single time He was tempted, Jesus quoted the Word of God, saying, "It is written ..." He overcame temptation through the Word of God because the Sword of the Spirit is powerful to cut through the lies of the devil and our own rationalizations and justifications. It is critical for a Christian to study and memorize the Word of God daily. "Your word I have hidden in my heart that I might not sin against You" (Psalm 119:11).

God's Word hidden in our hearts gives us ammunition against temptation when it surprises us with its opportunities contrary to the things of God. "Get behind Me, Satan! You are an offense to Me, for you are not mindful of the things of God, but the things of men" (Matthew 16:23).

To reiterate, "put on the Lord Jesus Christ, and make no provision for the flesh, to fulfill its lusts" (Romans 13:14). When a person becomes born again, they receive the power to overcome the sinful nature of their flesh and the bondage that was attached to that lifestyle. A Christian can daily feed their spiritual side and starve their fleshly side, so when temptation comes, their spiritual side is so much more powerful to withstand the demands of their flesh. Thus, we can be victorious in those moments. But if we fuel the flesh, then we will crumble under its power over us.

Jesus warns against adultery. He says if you encounter anything that causes you to stumble, turn from it. Cut it from your life. The price of stumbling in this area is too heavy to pay. In John 8:1-11, the Bible tells us of a woman caught in the act of adultery brought before Jesus. Scripture doesn't say where the man in question was. Perhaps this was a setup. However, Jesus saw through their plot, and the woman was spared. But the interesting thing about this scenario is that Jesus was the only righteous one among the crowd who could throw the first stone and the accused woman sat right in front of the only one who could condemn her. After everyone had left the scene, Jesus asked the woman to identify her accusers. He then dismissed her with the instruction to go and sin no more. Can you imagine what that was like for her to hear the Son of God forgive her? Jesus gave her a command, and whenever He gives us a command, He also gives us the ability to carry out his instructions.

If a Christian falls into sexual immorality intentionally, they must repent and turn from the sin that so easily befell them. The Bible instructs us to turn and live! Though Jesus forgives us, there may be some consequences, but better to be right with God than to continue to live in bondage and fear. May God help us to put on the Lord Jesus Christ, to make no provision for the flesh, and to walk in the victory He has provided. The Lord does not condemn us in these matters but admonishes us to repent, go forward, and sin no more.

THE SUBJECT OF DIVORCE

"Furthermore it has been said, 'Whoever divorces his wife, let him give her a certificate of divorce.' But I say to you that whoever divorces his wife for any reason except sexual immorality causes her to commit adultery; and whoever marries a woman who is divorced commits adultery" (Matthew 5:31-32).

Within His "Sermon on the Mount," Jesus addresses a subject that is both painful and controversial. Divorce was a growing problem, as it is today, that unravels the fabric of the family. Many have been personally affected by divorce. Some grew up in a broken home, spending time at parents' multiple locations, living with blended families, while others experienced the heartache of divorce from what they thought was a forever after marriage or marriages.

Statistics tell the sad story that anywhere from 50 to 60 percent of marriages end in divorce. And that statistic has made its way into the church. If each person could tell of their heartbreaking experience of divorce, many of the reasons and details that led to the ending of their marriages would greatly vary. Though some similarities would be apparent, the circumstances differ.

God's original intention, from the very beginning, when He

created man and woman and brought them together, was that there would be one man for one woman for life. He ordained marriage to last a lifetime. Yet, due to the choices made in the Garden of Eden, sin (separation from God) entered the world. Sin brought death.

In the Book of Proverbs, Solomon, who had some knowledge about women, gave some advice. "Drink water from your own cistern, flowing water from your own well. Should your springs be scattered abroad, streams of water in the streets? Let them be for yourself alone, and not for strangers with you. Let your fountain be blessed, and rejoice in the wife of your youth" (Proverbs 5:15-18 ESV). Solomon used the fountain, which has a source, as an illustration of marriage as a life source. This proverb tells us to invest in our marriage.

The Lord expresses His opinion of divorce in Malachi: "Because the Lord has been witness between you and the wife of your youth, with whom you have dealt treacherously; yet she is your companion and your wife by covenant. But did He not make them one, Having a remnant of the Spirit? And why one? He seeks godly offspring. Therefore, take heed to your spirit, and let none deal treacherously with the wife of his youth. For the Lord God of Israel says that He hates divorce, for it covers one's garment with violence," says the Lord of hosts. Therefore, take heed to your spirit that you do not deal treacherously" (Malachi 2:14-16).

God hates divorce due to its impact on the people involved, and the pain it produces, the burden it brings, the sorrow it spreads, and the repercussions and experience that affect everyone physically, emotionally, mentally, spiritually—in every way. The religious leaders of Jesus' day had developed their own teaching on the subject of divorce, and like so many of the laws of the Lord, they had established their own interpretation of the law on this matter.

Such as, if a man was going to divorce his wife, they emphasized that to make the sever of a marriage binding, he had to give her a certificate of divorcement. However, women were not allowed to divorce their husbands for any reason. In those days, women did not have many rights. While Jesus was in the midst of healing a throng of people, the Bible tells us that the religious leaders presented Him with a controversial question to which Jesus emphasizes and clarifies to a greater degree this subject of divorce. "The Pharisees also came to Him, testing Him, and saying to Him, "Is it lawful for a man to divorce his wife for just any reason?" (Matthew 19:3).

The Pharisees followed Jesus along with the people to test Him on the divorce issue as there were two sides. They intended to force Jesus to take one side over another and publicly discredit Him. In those days, many Jews considered divorce a virtue along the same lines as marriage. Among the rabbinical writings of the day, varying quotes circulated concerning a husband who was dealing with a difficult wife. One quote stated: "A bad wife is like leprosy to her husband. What is the remedy? Let him divorce her and be cured of his leprosy!" Another quote stated: "If a man has a bad wife, it is a religious duty to divorce her!" The controversy over divorce stemmed from the definition of uncleanness in an Old Testament passage: "When a man takes a wife and marries her, and it happens that she finds no favor in his eyes because he has found some uncleanness in her, and he writes her a certificate of divorce, puts it in her hand, and sends her out of his house" (Deuteronomy 24:1).

How did the Pharisees define uncleanness? The rabbis held varying opinions on what was meant by uncleanness. The liberal view interpreted by Rabbi Hillel defined unclean in a broad sense. He said that anything a man saw in his wife that he felt was unclean was grounds for divorce; such as, a spoiled dinner, brawling (as in hearing her voice from next door), speaking ill of her husband's parents, and wearing her hair down. The opposing view presented by Rabbi Akiva took the liberal approach further. He said if a man found a woman he deemed cleaner than his wife, he could write a bill of divorce. Rabbi Shammai held a stricter view that constituted uncleanness. He

FIELD GUIDE FOR YOUR FAITH: Sermon on the Mount

interpreted allowance of divorce under God's law to take into account marital impropriety, a shameful act, infidelity; or if a man discovered his wife was not pure before marriage.

However, neither view took into account that the act of adultery was not punishable by a bill of divorcement but by death. Instead, the dowry, an ancient form of alimony or a type of pre-nuptial agreement, was established. In summary, the religious leaders interpreted what Moses wrote as an obligation. But, once again, Jesus clarifies their misunderstanding and misinterpretation of the law.

> He answered, "Have you not read that he who created them from the beginning made them male and female, and said, 'Therefore a man shall leave his father and his mother and hold fast to his wife, and the two shall become one flesh?' So they are no longer two but one flesh. What therefore God has joined together, let not man separate." (Matthew 19:4-6 ESV).

Jesus pointed the Pharisees to Scripture, which, despite spending a great deal of their time studying, they appeared to have missed the true interpretation. Marriage is a work of God, but divorce is a work of man. But this did not satisfy the Pharisees who in response were ready with a follow-up question.

> "They said to Him, 'Why then did Moses command to give a certificate of divorce, and to put her away?' He said to them, 'Moses, because of the hardness of your hearts, permitted you to divorce your wives, but from the beginning it was not so'" (Matthew 19:7-8).

God did not give a command; rather, He permitted divorce because of the hardness of a man's heart. A marriage ends because of the hardness of heart of one party or both parties toward each other and God's Word. If we do not live according to what God says in His Word, our marriage has a good chance of ending. And Jesus, as the ultimate authority over marriage, clarifies the interpretation of the law concerning divorce. "And I say to you, whoever divorces his wife, except for sexual immorality, and marries another, commits adultery; and whoever marries her who is divorced commits adultery" (Matthew 19:9).

In context, Jesus was speaking to those advocating easy divorce. He was addressing those who thought they could put their wife away for any reason they deemed necessary (she wore her hair down, she burnt their eggs, she talked bad about their mother). He clarified that, except for sexual immorality, they were committing adultery if they divorced her.

The effects of divorce impact the next generation. Today there is a mindset that rather than marry and risk divorce, couples opt to live together without a marriage contract. Cohabitation seemingly offers the same benefits as that of a married couple, but this arrangement, supported by the devil, is unacceptable to God. From a biblical standpoint and God's perspective, if a Christian couple lives together in sexual union, they are living in sin and need to repent and get right with God.

Though statistics show a drop in divorce rates overall due to late-start marriages in Millennials, the drop is due to fewer marriages overall (Bloomberg, 2018). Couples are deciding to forego traditional marriage in favor of cohabitation. But God's plan is that a couple marries and He desires that divorce would not be an option. The reasons for divorce vary, but personal stories of those who ended their marriages and why have one thing in common: Restoration is possible with God because He does not deal in impossibilities. The Bible tells us in Ezekiel 37:1-6 that the Lord can breathe life into dry bones.

Though divorce is allowed for adultery, the Bible does not mandate this process. Marriages that survive infidelity embrace a key ingredient: Genuine repentance on the part of the person or persons who committed the offense against their spouse is visible by the fact that they have walked away from that other relationship, have repented to God, and are willing to wait as long as necessary for their spouse to be reconciled to them. Genuine repentance is not the justification of an action or blaming the other person. It's not setting a time limit on forgiveness from their spouse. Repentance is real when it is as notorious as the sin that was committed. There is a willingness, brokenness, and humility before God to do whatever it takes to restore that which was broken.

Another necessary component for restoration is that the person who has been offended and hurt must be willing and open to reconciling. Not because everyone else tells them they should but because it's what God is showing them to do. All that said, it is unwise for a woman to listen to counsel that would have them rush back into a relationship with a hateful, abusive, spiteful man or someone who is a liar, drug, or sex addict. If there is any chance of restoration, they should wait until such a man is completely broken and repentant. No one would want to put a woman and her children in harm's way. The Lord needs time to put things back together. In cases of desertion, God makes an allowance for permanent abandonment, whereas a prodigal husband or wife refuses to repent and return. "But if the unbeliever departs, let him depart; a brother or a sister is not under bondage in such cases. But God has called us to peace" (1 Corinthians 7:15).

It is well to mention that some prodigals provoke their spouses to file for divorce. They needle them to take the fall to try to pin the guilt on them because they do not want to appear culpable. But, in these cases, the spouse who is left is not under bondage.

After hearing these exceptions, some of Jesus' disciples reasoned that it might be better not to marry at all. But it is important to understand the purpose of marriage and God's plan for marriage to steer far away from ever becoming a statistic.

Some come into a marriage with the idea of being served. They have a false expectation at the altar that the person they are about to marry is going to meet all their needs. And when their bride or groom doesn't live up to that expectation, because they can't (no one can), suddenly disillusionment sets in and accusations fly. He isn't who I thought he was. She isn't what she appeared to be. This is not working out; I need to find someone else to fulfill my needs. Selfishness can create the worst damage to a marriage imaginable. Often, we don't realize how selfish we are until we marry. Marriage is a revelation! The wickedness of one's own heart is revealed as the two attempts to become one. God uses this revelation to change us into the person He wants us to become. Martin Luther said every man should have a wife if for nothing else but to keep him humble.

Bear in mind there are certain needs in our lives only God can fulfill. But some make the mistake of defining marriage as good as long as their spouse is meeting their expectations. When we realize we no longer have the capacity or reserve to tolerate our spouse's idiosyncrasies, imperfections that were once an endearment, hurt feelings can surface. People get defensive, which diminishes communication, heightens misunderstandings, provokes conflict, fuels anger and bitterness, which leads to unforgiveness and a downward spiral. Love becomes paralyzed.

For a successful marriage, we need to build a solid foundation in Christ. Jesus is the perfect role model for husbands because He loves perfectly. It is critical for a man to draw near to the Lord. As we draw near to Him, He draws near to us and performs in and through us the things we are incapable of performing. He makes us into the husbands and fathers who would otherwise fall short. Women who follow the example of Jesus by submitting to their husbands as unto the Lord are responsive to this undying love and fulfill their commitment to a marriage.

But couples who live separate lives that dis-include the Bible, fellowship and prayer are headed in the wrong direction. It is so important to invest in your spouse. The best way to produce a healthy, fruitful marriage is by making Jesus the first priority in our lives individually as believers. But if we neglect our intimate relationship with Jesus, then every other relationship is directly impacted. The Bible says a threefold cord is not easily broken (Ecclesiastes 4:12).

Marriage is like a garden. Gardens require careful consideration and daily care to water, weed, prune and trim plants for fragrant flowers to appear. For a garden to bloom in season, we must invest in proper care and feeding. A well-watered garden is a picture of a well cared for marriage. Husbands who love their wives as Christ loves the church and wives who submit to that love as the church submits to the Lord.

The union of marriage is God's plan, and under His plan, divorce is not an option. Rather, as Christians, we should divorce ourselves from the very idea of divorce. We need to honor our vows. For better or worse, richer or poorer. In sickness and health. Till death do us part. Those who have been hurt by divorce need to know that God can restore them.

8

OATHS

Within His "Sermon on the Mount" Jesus taught His disciples that unless righteousness exceeded that of the Pharisees and scribes, they would not enter the Kingdom of Heaven. No doubt when they were shocked upon hearing these words of Jesus; no one could measure up to the meticulous, dedicated righteousness displayed by the religious leaders.

These leaders went so far as to tithe their spices! As we previously learned, their spiritual model was greatly flawed. Their outward appearance was deceptive and hypocritical. Jesus gave His disciples six illustrations from the teachings of the law as described by the religious leaders, followed by a true interpretation of the law as originally written with God's actual intention.

"Again, you have heard that it was said to those of old, 'You shall not swear falsely, but shall perform to the Lord what you have sworn.' But I say to you, do not take an oath at all, either by heaven, for it is the throne of God, or by the earth, for it is his footstool, or by Jerusalem, for it is the city of the great King. And do not take an oath by your head, for you cannot make one hair white or black. Let what you say be simply 'Yes' or 'No'; anything more than this comes from evil" (Matthew 5:33-37 ESV).

Jesus referenced Scripture from the Old Testament on the taking of oaths according to a command given by God: "And you shall not swear by My name falsely, nor shall you profane the name of your God: I am the Lord" (Leviticus 19:12), and, "If a man makes a vow to the Lord, or swears an oath to bind himself by some agreement, he shall not break his word; he shall do according to all that proceeds out of his mouth" (Numbers 30:2).

The Lord wasn't opposed to people making vows, or declarations that they intended to fulfill a commitment, but if they made a commitment to the Lord, they should ensure they could indeed fulfill that commitment or not utter such an oath. "If you make a vow to the Lord your God, you shall not delay fulfilling it, for the Lord your God will surely require it of you, and you will be guilty of sin. But if you refrain from vowing, you will not be guilty of sin. You shall be careful to do what has passed your lips, for you have voluntarily vowed to the Lord your God what you have promised with your mouth" (Deuteronomy 23:21-23 ESV). It is important to be a person of your word, especially as it relates to the kingdom of God.

Within the Old Testament, we can observe different individuals who made vows to the Lord, invoking the Lord's Name. For example, after Abraham had rescued his nephew, Lot, who had been captured in war, and restored the land, the king of Sodom offered him a reward. "But Abram said to the king of Sodom, 'I have lifted my hand to the Lord, God Most High, Possessor of heaven and earth, that I would not take a thread or a sandal strap or anything that is yours, lest you should say, 'I have made Abram rich.' I will take nothing but what the young men have eaten, and the share of the men who went with me. Let Aner, Eshcol, and Mamre take their share.'" (Genesis 14:22-24 ESV). In other words, Abraham made a vow to the Lord that the victory belonged to Him, and he wasn't about to let anyone take credit for what God had done on his behalf.

David and Jonathan exemplify a friendship based on the love and worship of God. But King Saul, Jonathan's father, grew jealous of David's fame after he slew Goliath and started picking up spears with plans to pin David to the wall! On the other hand, Jonathan, who was in line to take over his father's throne, saw God's anointing upon his friend and gave David allegiance before he became king. Jonathan gladly stepped aside and made a covenant with David.

The standard protocol for a king about to take the throne was to eradicate all of his descendants so no one would be able to challenge his position. But David and Jonathan had such a close-knit friendship that they made a binding agreement in the name of the Lord. "Then Jonathan said to David, "Go in peace, since we have both sworn in the name of the Lord, saying, 'May the Lord be between you and me, and between your descendants and my descendants, forever'" (1 Samuel 20:42 ESV). Making an oath or vow in the name of the Lord is serious and defines one's character, as David writes in Psalm 15.

In Psalm 50:14, the Bible says, "Offer to God thanksgiving, and pay your vows to the Most High." During times of trouble, we often turn to psalms. "I will come into your house with burnt offerings, I will perform my vows to you, that which my lips uttered and my mouth promised when I was in trouble" (Psalm 66:13-14 ESV). How many people today make vows, especially when they're in trouble? *Lord, I promise … if you get me out of this … I will never do that again! Lord, please deliver me from this bad decision that I made, this messed up relationship … if You could just change my direction … if you get me out of this prison cell, here's what I'm going to do.*

The Bible tells us Jacob had ripped his brother off from the family birthright when Esau, who despised his birthright, made an oath with his brother for a bowl of lentil soup. Then, Rebekah encouraged Jacob to deceive his dying father Isaac to install the family blessing upon him over Esau. Jacob had to flee the wrath of his brother for robbing him of his rightful blessing. On his way, Jacob dreamt of a ladder with angels ascending and descending (Jacob's Ladder), and the Lord spoke to him (Genesis 28:13-15). The next day, Jacob worshipped God and poured oil on the rock that was his pillow to make a vow to the Lord. Here Jacob is in trouble making a vow to God (Genesis 28:16-22).

Jonah is another example of someone who when in trouble, made a vow to God. This prophet ran from God's calling by boarding a ship headed in the opposite direction of where the Lord had called him. He was eventually thrown overboard, and a big fish swallowed him. After three days inside the belly of the fish, Jonah cried out to the Lord for deliverance (Jonah 2:7-9).

God caused the fish to vomit Jonah onto the shores of Nineveh to preach salvation to a dying people, and a great revival followed.

Solomon wrote in the Book of Ecclesiastes on the subject of making a vow, and he said: "When you make a vow to God, do not delay to pay it; For He has no pleasure in fools. Pay what you have vowed—Better not to vow than to vow and not pay. Do not let your mouth cause your flesh to sin, nor say before the messenger of God that it was an error. Why should God be angry at your excuse and destroy the work of your hands?" (Ecclesiastes 5:4-6 ESV).

Then there was Jephthah, who made a foolish vow. God didn't tell him to make a vow; He had already promised Jephthah a victory in battle. "And Jephthah made a vow to the Lord, and said, 'If You will indeed deliver the people of Ammon into my hands, then it will be that whatever comes out of the doors of my house to meet me, when I return in peace from the people of Ammon, shall surely be the Lord's, and I will offer it up as a burnt offering'" (Judges 11:30-31).

Following Jephthah's return from victory, his only child, a daughter, was there to greet him, with a tambourine as was the custom. Suddenly, all the cheers and excitement from victory turn to sorrow and anguish. His daughter went into the hills and mourned her virginity as now she would never be able to marry as a result of her father's foolish and unnecessary vow. Her life became a tremendous sacrifice.

The Bible records that God Himself made a vow. The writer of

Hebrews gives us a commentary concerning when Abraham went up Mount Moriah to offer up Isaac, his only son, as a sacrifice and God held him back (see Genesis 22). "For when God made a promise to Abraham, since he had no one greater by whom to swear, he swore by himself, saying, 'Surely I will bless you and multiply you'" (Hebrews 6:13-14 ESV). Abraham knew God would fulfill His promise because the Lord gave him His Word. And there is no one higher than God. He was sure to fulfill that promise.

We come to realize that the Lord gave the opportunity to fulfill an oath or to give a vow to validate the strength in one's commitment. But the teaching found in the law we have been referencing had been tampered with by the religious leaders. Like so many of the other laws, they had tampered with the law of God. The religious leaders found ways to sidestep an obligation by using an oath. And they were using this "loophole" in such a way that it wasn't binding (Matthew 23:16-22).

Essentially, the religious leaders had created a loophole for themselves that alleviated them from remaining true to their vow but still made them appear to be righteous on the outside. This loophole made them culturally accepted. It made them look spiritually astute and righteous in the sight of the people. Yet they had no intention of fulfilling the true law, of performing that which they said they would do. In light of this deceptive use of oaths, and their twisting of the law used to suit their own purposes, Jesus instructed them concerning oaths.

> Again you have heard that it was said to those of old, 'You shall not swear falsely, but shall perform to the Lord what you have sworn.' But I say to you, do not take an oath at all, either by heaven, for it is the throne of God, or by the earth, for it is his footstool, or by Jerusalem, for it is the city of the great King. And do not take an oath by your head, for you cannot make one hair white or black. Let what you say be simply 'Yes' or 'No'; anything more than this comes from evil" (Matthew 5:33-37 ESV).

The culture says one thing, but Jesus says something else. The ways of the Lord are contrary to the ways of the world. Society may deem a practice acceptable, but as Christians, we are accountable to God because He is the ultimate authority in our lives. Furthermore, Jesus says, "My sheep hear My voice, and I know them, and they follow Me" (John 10:27).

Jesus sums up His statement on this part of the law by saying, "But let your 'Yes' be 'Yes,' and your 'No,' 'No.' For whatever is more than these is from the evil one" (Matthew 5:37). In other words, be a person of your word. Don't think you can say you can swear by the temple but didn't swear by the gold in the temple; therefore, it is not valid. Don't partially lie and call it truth; a half-truth is still a lie. When someone is caught in a lie or you find out later they did not tell you the whole truth, it becomes difficult to trust that person because we build relationships on trust. If someone can lie to your face, you are left wondering what else they have kept from you. When a person lies consistently, they can actually begin to believe their lies as truth. Their bald-faced lies and storytelling can mock the truth so much that it becomes hard to tell fact from fiction.

Judas Iscariot is a prime example of this behavior in the New Testament. This disciple was so good at lying that none of the other disciples knew of his plan to betray Jesus. The Bible says, "You desire truth in the inward parts, and in the hidden part You will make me to know wisdom" (Psalm 51:6), and, "Lying lips are an abomination to the Lord, but those who deal truthfully are His delight" (Proverbs 12:22).

In the next illustration, Jesus points to the law of retaliation.

9

THE LAW OF RETALIATION: AN EYE FOR AN EYE

The law of retaliation is one of the most misunderstood and misinterpreted portions of the "Sermon on the Mount."

> "You have heard that it was said, 'An eye for an eye and a tooth for a tooth.' But I tell you not to resist an evil person. But whoever slaps you on your right cheek, turn the other to him also. If anyone wants to sue you and take away your tunic, let him have your cloak also. And whoever compels you to go one mile, go with him two. Give to him who asks you, and from him who wants to borrow from you do not turn away" (Matthew 5:38-42).

Some have come to wrong conclusions regarding what Jesus is saying in these verses. Men like Tolstoy, Gandhi, and others have misunderstood and misapplied this passage, going so far as to claim we should not have a police or military force. When interpreting Scripture, it is necessary to compare Scripture with Scripture. If our interpretation is not clear with other parts of Scripture, then there is something wrong with the interpretation, because the Word of God is inerrant and God does not contradict Himself. In this illustration, Jesus is talking about the righteousness of the Pharisees by comparison to the righteousness of His Kingdom. In so doing, He references the Old Testament; specifically, how the Book of Exodus states the law.

> "If men fight, and hurt a woman with child, so that she gives birth prematurely, yet no harm follows, he shall surely be punished accordingly as the woman's husband imposes on him; and he shall pay as the judges determine. But if any harm follows, then you shall give life for life, eye for eye, tooth for tooth, hand for hand, foot for foot, burn for burn, wound for wound, stripe for stripe" (Exodus 21:22-25).

Again, according to the law, Leviticus 24 states: "If a man causes disfigurement of his neighbor, as he has done, so shall it be done to him—fracture for fracture, eye for eye, tooth for tooth; as he has caused disfigurement of a man, so shall it be done to him" (vv. 19-20); and, "Your eye shall not pity: life shall be for life, eye for eye, tooth for tooth, hand for hand, foot for foot" (Deuteronomy 19:21).

Primarily, this principle was in the context of civil authority to apply when making a judgment in a court of law. This law was put in place so that the punishment would fit and not exceed the crime. Designed to guard against vengeance, revenge, and violent revenge, this law also served as a warning to deter crime. If we're honest, our natural human tendency wants revenge. We want to take justice a step further and are not satisfied with less. If someone is hurt, their natural inclination tends toward hurting the other person twice as much. However, the Lord restricts us in His Word. The Lord says vengeance belongs to Him. The law wasn't put in place by God for us to take the law into our own hands.

God put a provision in place, but the religious leaders tampered with His intent, thus perverting the law. The problem arose when the rabbis, teachers, and Pharisees taught that the law was given as a license for people to exact justice if they so desired. The leaders presented the law as a right for people to take the role of judge, jury, and executioner. They taught that a person had a legal right to settle the score if accosted in any way and to do to the offender precisely what the offender did to them by taking personal vengeance against them. An eye for an eye wasn't a limitation on the law but an opportunity for revenge.

Jesus clarifies that their teaching differs from the righteousness of the kingdom, and Jesus didn't just point this out, He also lived it out. His life is a perfect example of God's law in action. Jesus said, "But I tell you not to resist an evil person. But whoever slaps you on your right cheek, turn the other to him also. If anyone wants to sue you and take away your tunic, let him have your cloak also. And whoever compels you to go one mile, go with him two. Give to him who asks you, and from him who wants to borrow from you do not turn away" (Matthew 5:39-42).

It is important when studying a passage of Scripture to keep in mind the interpretation according to the rest of Scripture. Jesus is not implying that we should not have civil authority, police officers, or that we should not fight against evil within the world. Nor is He saying we should let evil run its course as this would be inconsistent with the rest of Scripture. The law has been put in place for a reason, and the authority that holds those who break the law accountable are put in place by God. Paul tells us this clearly in Romans 13:1-4.

If there were no written laws to keep society accountable, people would run wild. Societies where lawlessness rules are followed by the chaos of death and destruction. For our protection, civil laws must govern nations. Peter tells us, "Be subject for the Lord's sake to every human institution, whether it be to the emperor as supreme, or to governors as sent by him to punish those who do evil and to praise those who do good. For this is the will of God, that by doing good you should put to silence the ignorance of foolish people" (1 Peter 2:13-15 ESV).

We are called to be law-abiding citizens and as Christians good examples. There are times when we need to fight against governors and others in legislation by voting. The Constitution says this country is run by the people and for the people. We should take advantage of the privilege and opportunity to take a stand against evil practices for the glory of God. If you see something evil in the governmental setting or a regime that rises to oppress its people, it is a duty to stand up for what is right.

Think of the lawless regimes that rose to power, such as Hitler, and how we fought against those horrors of war and evil. The Bible also talks to us about resisting evil in the church. Such as when Jesus entered the Temple and overturned the tables because of the corruption that had entered. Vendors had turned the House of Prayer into a den of thieves, taking advantage of the people.

Paul wrote to the church in Corinth; members of the congregation were suing each other in front of unbelievers, thus tarnishing the testimony of Christ. In this context, the religious leaders were misconstruing God's law and taking matters into their own hands. "I say this to your shame. Is it so, that there is not a wise man among you, not even one, who will be able to judge between his brethren? But brother goes to law against brother, and that before unbelievers!" (1 Corinthians 6:5-6). Again, the leaders found a loophole but as Jesus clarifies each passage concerning the law in the Old Testament that references an eye for an eye deals with the civil system, the trial and sentencing always responsible by its appointed judges to meet the crime. Jesus reveals the heart of the matter and clarifies that the law of retaliation was not intended for personal offenses.

In the Jewish culture, a slap across the face is a sign of utter disregard and disrespect and is considered degrading and undignified. While in Jerusalem, the Apostle Paul challenged the high priest who had him unlawfully struck in the face. "And looking intently at the council, Paul said, 'Brothers, I have lived my life before God in all good conscience up to this day.' And the high priest Ananias commanded those who stood by him to strike him on the mouth. Then Paul said to him, 'God is going to strike you, you whitewashed wall! Are you sitting to judge me according to the law, and yet contrary to the law you order me to be struck?'" (Acts 23:1-3 ESV).

When we are personally struck, slighted, insulted or disrespected (and all have been disrespected and have disrespected others), at that moment we have a decision to make on how to respond. Though self-defense is our natural response, Jesus says to turn the other cheek, to walk away from personal attacks. Don't respond. Just let it go.

During His ministry, though Jesus was slighted repeatedly, He responded in love, grace, and mercy. The Lord sets the bar, and we all have far to go to measure up to His standard. Peter writes that suffering wrongfully for good and entrusting the wrongdoing to the Lord is commendable. God takes notice of our sufferings, and He is a righteous judge (2 Peter 2:18-24).

ON LAWSUITS

"If anyone wants to sue you and take away your tunic, let him have your cloak also. And whoever compels you to go one mile, go with him two. Give to him who asks you, and from him who wants to borrow from you do not turn away" (Matthew 5:40-42). In addressing legal issues, Jesus is not implying that if you are taken to court unlawfully, you cannot hire an attorney or a defense team. We live in a fallen world and some attempt unlawful activities, which gives us no other alternative but to seek legal channels.

Concerning going the extra mile, in those days Rome occupied Israel, and there was a strong military presence. Rome required citizens to comply with specific laws. For instance, a soldier could intrude upon anyone at any time and order them to carry their bags over a certain distance. Jesus' response to this intrusion was to go above and beyond the requirement. To go the extra mile. The opposite of our natural reaction to an imposition.

The Bible tells us, "A soft answer turns away wrath, but a harsh word stirs up anger" (Proverbs 15:1), and, "By long forbearance a ruler is persuaded, and a gentle tongue breaks a bone" (Proverbs 25:15). The world does not expect a gentle response to an unkind gesture or inconvenient burden, but such a response can make an impact on the outcome. As Christians, Jesus encourages us to take the high road, which is the opposite of our human nature, and to live as unto the Lord.

LOVE YOUR ENEMY

The religious leaders installed certain parameters toward "enemies" but Jesus addresses these "obligations" by correcting the treatment of and attitude toward humanity overall.

> "You have heard that it was said, 'You shall love your neighbor and hate your enemy.' But I say to you, love your enemies and pray for those who persecute you, so that you may be sons of your Father who is in heaven. For he makes his sun rise on the evil and on the good, and sends rain on the just and on the unjust. For if you love those who love you, what reward do you have? Do not even the tax collectors do the same? And if you greet only your brothers, what more are you doing than others? Do not even the Gentiles do the same? You therefore must be perfect, as your heavenly Father is perfect" (Matthew 5:43-48 ESV).

It is difficult for most people to love an enemy, but Jesus exemplified how to respond to hostilities. He gives a command here to love, bless, do good to, and pray for those who curse, hate, and spitefully use and persecute us. This is not the natural response to an enemy. Jesus describes the kind of love that characterizes a Christian: "I say to you, love your enemies and pray for those who persecute you" (v. 44).

1. He says to love them. Without love we have nothing: "And if I have prophetic powers, and understand all mysteries and all knowledge, and if I have all faith, so as to remove mountains, but have not love, I am nothing if I give away all I have, and if I deliver up my body to be burned, but have not love, I gain nothing" (1 Corinthians 13:2-3).
2. Bless and do good to them. God shows us how to bless others. One way is not to talk about or respond to their actions. Bless them in the name of the Lord. Be an example of the love of Jesus.
3. Pray for them. Prayer has the power to change things and to change us. When we pray for our enemies, for those who hurt us, Jesus softens our hearts and reveals that we, too, are sinners in need of grace and forgiveness. How can we not forgive others when God forgives us? Spurgeon said, "Prayer is the forerunner of mercies."

John 3:16 tells us of His merciful intentions: "For God so loved the world that He gave His only begotten Son, that whoever believes in Him should not perish but have everlasting life." Even as Jesus hung on the cross, He stated, "Father, forgive them, for they know not what they do" (Luke 23:34). We may not understand God's love, but we can look to Jesus as our model. It is not difficult to love someone who loves us, but those who oppose us challenge our faith and ability to love them at all. Jesus shows us that grace to love those who do not love us in return distinguishes us as belonging to Christ with the characteristics and attributes of the Father, for God is love.

Matthew reports that when one of the scribes, a lawyer, asked Jesus about the greatest commandment, "He said to him, 'You shall love the Lord your God with all your heart and with all your soul and with all your mind.' This is the great and first commandment. And a second is like it: 'You shall love your neighbor as yourself.' On these two commandments depend all the Law and the Prophets" (Matthew 22:37-40 ESV). This type of love for enemies is reminiscent of Joseph loving and caring for his brothers though they wrecked a good portion of his life. Also, one thinks of David, who let Saul live even though he had every opportunity to take him out. Acts records another example of a saint choosing not to retaliate: "And they stoned Stephen as he was calling on God and saying, 'Lord Jesus, receive my spirit.' Then he knelt down and cried out with a loud voice, 'Lord, do not charge them with this sin.' And when he had said this, he fell asleep" (Acts 7:59-60).

As Jesus hung on the cross, the multitude jeered at Him that if He was truly the Messiah to come down from the cross, to save Himself. Though we are incapable of living up to His model (especially to what Jesus accomplished on the cross), mapped out in the "Sermon on the Mount," we can look to the Holy Spirit to empower us with the strength to respond in the spirit and not in our flesh. All of us are a work in progress. May God help us to embrace the characteristics of our Heavenly Father that we may genuinely represent Him as His sons and daughters. For when we lay down our lives for friends and enemies, therein lies an incredible opportunity to identify with and become more like Jesus.

10

CHARITY

H aving addressed the inward relationship to the law, in chapter six of Matthew, Jesus begins to preach on the outward expression of their relationship to God. That is, how are we to live in the midst of this world in light of what we believe? Jesus brings three areas to the forefront that were extremely important to the religious life of the Jews: giving, praying and fasting.

> "Take heed that you do not do your charitable deeds before men, to be seen by them. Otherwise you have no reward from your Father in heaven. Therefore, when you do a charitable deed, do not sound a trumpet before you as the hypocrites do in the synagogues and in the streets, that they may have glory from men. Assuredly, I say to you, they have their reward. But when you do a charitable deed, do not let your left hand know what your right hand is doing, that your charitable deed may be in secret; and your Father who sees in secret will Himself reward you openly" (Matthew 6:1-4).

GIVING

When Jesus uses the words "take heed," He's issuing a warning to be on guard against a very subtle, yet real temptation everyone encounters. That is, the temptation to serve the Lord in a way that brings glory to ourselves. To be seen and applauded. There is a desire within each of us for acceptance by others. In some way, we want others to notice us. And in our world of social media today, this fact is evident. People communicate through social media. Though social media is fine in its proper place, we would be wise to check our motivation. There appears to be a difference between posting and boasting. It's a very fine line, and not too many people post about bad days that include mess-ups and mishaps. Instead, most report their highlight reels. They post good times and how they would like to be known.

Jesus warns us about giving to others to boost our visibility. The phrase "charitable deeds" can refer to any outward active mercy toward someone else as in a good deed. Primarily, charitable deeds deal with giving financially, but a charitable person has many different expressions. Jesus begins by telling His disciples the way not to give. He issued a warning about the poor example modeled for them to follow. "Take heed that you do not do your charitable deeds before men, to be seen by them. Otherwise, you have no reward from your Father in heaven" (Matthew 6:1).

In other words, if you're going to give charitably or serve in some capacity, don't do it for the sake of being seen. The phrase "seen by men" is related to a term where we get the word "theatre." Putting on a show for the applause of others. The religious leaders of Jesus' day practiced good deeds on the world stage to display their "righteousness" to be recognized and commended by others. This behavior inflated their spiritual pride and was not considered truly righteous in the sight of God.

Jesus tells them, "Therefore, when you do a charitable deed, do not sound a trumpet before you as the hypocrites do in the synagogues and in the streets, that they may have glory from men. Assuredly, I say to you, they have their reward" (Matthew 6:2). The religious leaders would draw attention to themselves. Whether they hired a band to go before them on the way to the synagogue to alert people they were about to give charitably or carried a trumpet along the way, they wanted everybody to know of their good deeds. In his commentary of this portion of the "Sermon on the Mount," Charles Spurgeon wrote, "To stand with a penny in one hand and a trumpet in the other is the posture of hypocrisy."

Though their motivation was to impress the people of their good deeds in the open, Jesus said serving the Lord is not a platform for others to focus on us. He says not to give in this way nor promote our good deeds in the open for the possibility of receiving glory from others because any reward received on earth is temporary. Instead, we are to serve in such a way as to be seen by our Heavenly Father. Why is this so important? Why does Jesus emphasize giving in this manner? Jesus encourages us to live to serve God because the reward we receive from the Father is eternal. How many eternal rewards have we forfeited for the sake of temporary rewards?

Some of the rabbinical teachings of the day stated that to give charitably could actually save one from death and atone for their sins. Many felt it was easier for the rich to be saved rather than the poor because they could buy their way into heaven. But Jesus clarifies that this was nothing more than a sign of hypocrisy. The word hypocrite is a word that means "a play-actor." In theatre, the audience expects an actor to get into character to play a part in the drama. The actor's job is to embody someone else convincingly. However, when we enter the house of the Lord, we don't expect to see somebody play-acting. We would be surprised if someone placed a mask on their face to pretend to be someone else. There's a higher expectation for authenticity in the church. When a person strikes up the band or blows a trumpet in church to draw attention to themselves, in effect a work of the flesh, they are drawing attention away from God. God does not honor or reward a work of the flesh.

In the early church, when Barnabas gave financial support, and the body of Christ was encouraged, Ananias and Sapphira sought to give charitably as well. But this couple gave to the church deceitfully for recognition. God knew of their feigned religious hypocrisy and pre-meditated deception. "But Peter said, "Ananias, why has Satan filled your heart to lie to the Holy Spirit and keep back part of the price of the land for yourself? While it remained, was it not your own? And after it was sold, was it not in your own control? Why have you conceived this thing in your heart? You have not lied to men but to God" (Acts 5:3-4).

Jesus clarifies what a member who serves the kingdom of God looks like, "But when you do a charitable deed, do not let your left hand know what your right hand is doing, that your charitable deed may be in secret; and your Father who sees in secret will Himself reward you openly" (Matthew 6:3-4). Do not let your left hand know what your right hand is doing. The right hand was the hand of action! When you serve, do so discreetly without drawing attention to yourself to what you are doing! Here Jesus is addressing the unseen inclination to self-congratulate oneself. I'm so charitable, and nobody else knows how good I am. This is called self-acknowledgment. Wow, I am sure that act of mercy just added about five jewels to my coming crown. If we don't control our thoughts, self-congratulations can overshadow the goodness for which God wants to reward us.

To the best of our ability, when we give financially or serve the kingdom of God in other ways, we do so discreetly to avoid bringing attention to ourselves. Of course, there are times when we do things in the name of the Lord, and people are around, observing. It is impossible to serve incognito as though on a secret mission so no one can see what we're doing. Nothing to see here. Move on.

Yet we don't want to be weird about serving. The important thing is that we don't allow our flesh to turn an act of mercy into spiritual pride, which leads to hypocrisy and pretending. We might ask about the desire in our hearts, whether a serving opportunity is for recognition or we truly want to serve as unto the Lord. As much as we struggle to give all the glory to God, in truth, we have a common battle with the flesh in that a little glory for ourselves is sure to creep in. Though from the moment we are born, the natural tendency is to say "look at me" as we age that outward call for recognition becomes subtler with such phrases as "Check this out!" or "Yea, we give to that ministry and have for years."

If we seek recognition from people, we can end up forfeiting God's blessing, which is so much better than what the world can offer. "Your Father who sees in secret will Himself reward you openly" (Matthew 6:4). As we do things unto the Lord for His glory, He sees that. He knows what nobody else knows. He sees what we give and how we serve. We can never out-give God. The Lord is so generous and faithful toward us. God is so good.

Mark talks about when Jesus was actually in the area of the treasury, observing how people were giving to the Lord. "Many rich people put in large sums. And a poor widow came and put in two small copper coins, which make a penny. And he called his disciples to him and said to them, 'Truly, I say to you, this poor widow has put in more than all those who are contributing to the offering box. For they all contributed out of their abundance, but she out of her poverty has put in everything she had, all she had to live on'" (Mark 12:41-44 ESV). Jesus, whose value system differs from the world's economic system, observes a person's situation. People look at how much a person gives while Jesus looks at the heart behind the giving. He observed that the widow gave more than anyone else because she gave from her poverty, which was a sacrifice on her part. Jesus honors how we give.

We can easily overlook an important point concerning the passage in Matthew 6:3, "But when you do a charitable deed, do not let your left hand know what your right hand is doing." The point is found in the word when. Please notice Jesus does not say to his disciples, "if."

Therefore, Jesus is implying to when one serves, and not if one serves, as part of a follower of Christ. Charity follows the example of Christ, which is evident in John 3:16, "For God so loved the world that He gave His only begotten Son."

Our God is a charitable and generous God. When asked what constitutes generosity unto the Lord, Jesus defines charitable behavior on behalf of God. "And the King will answer and say to them, 'Assuredly, I say to you, inasmuch as you did it to one of the least of these, My brethren, you did it to Me'" (Matthew 25:40).

Some are only on the receiving end of charity, which is unfortunate because when we give there are a tremendous joy and reward with a blessing from God that follows. There are three basic principles relative to giving. First, as we extend our gratitude to God, giving becomes an act of worship as a way of life. Our very act of worship is a reasonable service. All that we are belongs to the Lord, and everything we own is on loan from Him. Giving, therefore, is our response to all that the Lord has bestowed upon us. Second, giving is an individual matter between our Lord Jesus and us. The Bible says for each person to give as they purpose in their hearts. Third, giving is a consistent privilege to give back to the Lord as He gives to us. In this context, the giving is anonymous. But the real reason we give is to invest in the kingdom of God. As theologian William Barclay said, "The need awakens the desire that cannot be stilled."

Jesus said, "Do not lay up for yourselves treasures on earth, where moth and rust destroy and where thieves break in and steal; but lay up for yourselves treasures in heaven, where neither moth nor rust destroys and where thieves do not break in and steal. For where your treasure is, there your heart will be also" (Matthew 6:19-21).

THE PRIVILEGE OF PRAYER

From His "Sermon on the Mount," Jesus talks about the privilege of prayer. He tells His disciples how not to pray: "And when you pray, you shall not be like the hypocrites. For they love to pray standing in the synagogues and on the corners of the streets, that they may be seen by men. Assuredly, I say to you, they have their reward" (Matthew 6:5).

Our relationship with the Father is made possible through Jesus Christ. Previously, we were separated from God because of sin, but Jesus bridged the gap when He died in our place. Once we are born again into God's family, as a child of God, we have access to the throne. The Bible tells us, "Let us, therefore, come boldly to the throne of grace, that we may obtain mercy and find grace to help in time of need" (Hebrews 4:16).

It is crucial for us to grasp that God loves us and longs to hear from us. His door is always open for us to enter. He is never too busy, and He is always available and accessible. Prayer is a privilege that has been given to every believer by our Father in heaven. "But without faith, it is impossible to please Him, for he who comes to God must believe that He is and that He is a rewarder of those who diligently seek Him" (Hebrews 11:6).

The religious leaders of Jesus' day had the responsibility of teaching the people God's Word. They also served as a pattern for the people to follow God. But rather than living according to God's Word, they found ways around God's Word. They developed interpretations and traditions, which they held in higher esteem than God's law, and established a religious existence that appeared respectable on the outside. However, on the inside, their "religion" was much different. Jesus saw through the façade of the Pharisees and, therefore, taught His disciples the true meaning of God's law from the very beginning. He spoke with clarity and authority.

One of the areas Jesus addressed was the practice and privilege of prayer. The religious leaders prayed with vain repetition instead of sincere devotion. Conversely, Jesus encouraged His disciples to pray in a secret place, and He said that the Father would then reward them openly. He instructed them not to pray with vain repetition or ineffective cadence but to pray with understanding. He reminded them that their Father knew what they needed even before they asked. The Bible tells us, "Now this is the confidence that we have in Him, that if we ask anything according to His will, He hears us" (1 John 5:14).

Many problems occurred among the religious leaders in the area of prayer. For many, prayer had become nothing more than a mechanical ritual. They set their petitions in such a way all they had to do was recite the lines and exit. These prayer lines were repeated over and over again without regard to content, and actual dialogue did not take place with anyone. They didn't need to think about what they were praying and also prescribed prayers written out in a catalog for specific occasions. Rather than communicate with the Creator of the universe, the religious leaders were merely going through the motions.

Furthermore, the religious leaders felt that lengthier prayers were more powerful. The longer one prayed, the more powerful their prayers, and to be more effective, it was essential to lengthen prayers, but Jesus said to beware of the scribes who do such things because they will receive a greater condemnation (Mark 12:38-40).

Dwight L. Moody wrote, "A man who prays much in private will make short prayers in public," and it is attributed to Charles Spurgeon, "The man who prays long in public probably doesn't pray very much in private." The point is that prayer is a personal dialog with the Lord and not something to spew out in public to show everyone that you are a person of prayer.

Moreover, Jesus mentions that the religious leaders prayed "not to be heard by God but to be seen by men." The Jews would pray, and specifically the religious leaders, three times a day: at 9:00 in the morning, at noon, and at 3:00 in the afternoon. The scribes prayed in the synagogue; however, if they were en route to the synagogue, and happened to be running late, they would pray on the spot in the street, which was a major interchange, a thoroughfare where everyone could observe their piety. In Luke's gospel, Jesus told a parable about two men who went to pray—one a religious leader and the other a publican (Luke 18:9-13).

The Pharisee paraded his accomplishments before God while the tax collector humbled himself in the sight of the Lord, to which Jesus replied: "I tell you, this man went down to his house justified rather than the other; for everyone who exalts himself will be humbled, and he who humbles himself will be exalted" (Luke 18:14).

Jesus received the prayers of one and rejected the prayers of the other. He was looking at the heart behind the person who was praying. We don't need to put on a show or get all olde English in speech, use a "prayer voice" to speak with the Lord or raise the volume as if God were deaf. Next, in the "Sermon on the Mount," Jesus tells His disciples how to pray. "But you, when you pray, go into your room, and when you have shut your door, pray to your Father who is in the secret place; and your Father who sees in secret will reward you openly" (Matthew 6:6).

As Christians, we have an open line of communication with God. Jesus says to seek seclusion and solitude with God to drown out the distractions in the world. When we meet God in the secret place, or a quiet spot, we can focus on spending uninterrupted time in prayer with the Lord. Jesus taught His disciples to pray with understanding.

Though some grow up saying the same bedtime prayer day in and day out, such as, "Now I lay me down to sleep, I pray the Lord my soul to keep; if I should die before I wake, I pray the Lord my soul to take." Or the more comforting mealtime prayer we all pray at one time or another, "Lord, bless this food to our bodies," Jesus assures us that He knows everything about us and all our needs before we even seek Him in prayer. "And when you pray, *do* not use vain repetitions as the heathen do. For they think that they will be heard for their many words. Therefore, do not be like them. For your Father knows the things you have need of before you ask Him" (Matthew 6:7-8).

Jesus knows how our day went, about our victories and disappointments. We can say things to the Lord that we wouldn't say to anybody else. Though He knows our needs beforehand, we can still approach Him, and though His way out or way in may differ from our expectations, we can trust Him in all things. The truth of the matter is when we pray we don't always know what is best. Though we may try to convince God about a certain outcome, ultimately the Lord knows what we need and what is best for us.

God is not reluctant to hear from us. He welcomes our prayers in the same way as we attend to our own children so we can meet their needs. Consider how the will of God is accomplished in heaven. *What's going on in heaven right now? What does the perfect will of God look like in heaven at this moment?* John recorded a preview of heaven in the Book of Revelation: "And every creature which is in heaven and on the earth and under the earth and such as are in the sea, and all that are in them, I heard saying: 'Blessing and honor and glory and power Be to Him who sits on the throne, and to the Lamb, forever and ever!'" (Revelation 5:13).

Another glimpse reveals: "Then the seventh angel sounded: And there were loud voices in *heaven*, saying, 'The kingdoms of this world have become *the kingdoms* of our Lord and of His Christ, and He shall reign forever and ever!'" (Revelation 11:15).

In the interim for Christians, prayer is our privilege and blessing. The Bible encourages us to pray for one another but seeking God in prayer should be our first resort. We can run to others to tell them our story as it unfolds, or we can run to God in heaven and invite Him into the situation before reaching out to others. After giving His disciples directions about how *not* to pray, Jesus gave them a model prayer with elements on how to pray.

12

THE LORD'S PRAYER TEACHES US TO PRAY

Throughout His earthly ministry, Jesus was found praying, rising early before daybreak, seeking the will of the Father. The disciples had seen and observed the impact that Jesus' personal prayer life had on His everyday life. So much so that at one point, they came to Him and said, "Lord, would you teach us how to pray?"

If Jesus found it necessary to rise early and pray, it is inherent for believers today to do the same, to become people of prayer, seeking God's will for their lives. Timothy Keller said, "The basic purpose of prayer is not to bend God's will to mine, but to mold my will into His."

Many have referred to Matthew for "The Lord's Prayer" or the "Our Father." This prayer was not designed for His disciples to repeat over and over because Jesus had just told them not to pray with vain repetition. Rather than a prescribed prayer or a vain repetition, "The Lord's Prayer" served as a model to the disciples on how to pray. This "Disciples' Prayer" illustrates some key elements to consider when one prays. Notice that the first stanzas of this prayer contain three petitions concerning God, while the later lines speak to us.

> Our Father in heaven,
> Hallowed be Your name.
> Your kingdom come.
> Your will be done
> On earth as it is in heaven.
> Give us this day our daily bread.
> And forgive us our debts,
> As we forgive our debtors.
> And do not lead us into temptation,
> But deliver us from the evil one.
> For Yours is the kingdom and the power
> and the glory forever. Amen (Matthew 6:9-13).

VERSE 9: THE PERSON OF GOD – ACKNOWLEDGING A HOLY GOD

This prayer begins by acknowledging a holy God: "Our Father in heaven, *hallowed* be Your Name." Prayer, and the opportunity to pray, is based on relationship. A person cannot have a prayer life apart from a relationship with God. The first prayer we need to pray is for God to save us from our sins. Once we receive salvation, we are part of the family of God. "For you did not receive the spirit of bondage again to fear, but you received the Spirit of adoption by whom we cry out, 'Abba, Father'" (Romans 8:15).

It was a revelation for a Jew to refer to God as "our Father." The word "Abba" is the equivalent of saying "Daddy." In Israel, small boys call after their fathers using this term. The Bible tells us that we have been adopted into His kingdom, into the family of God, and we are referred to as His children. We have been given the privilege of being called the children of God. As a result, we have the liberty to speak to God as our Father and we know that He hears us.

Philip asked Jesus to show him the Father, to which Jesus replied, "Have I been with you so long, and yet you have not known Me,

Philip? He who has seen Me has seen the Father; so how can you say, 'Show us the Father?' Do you not believe that I am in the Father and the Father in Me? The words that I speak to you I do not speak on My own authority; but the Father who dwells in Me does the works" (John 14:9-10). Everything we want to know about the Father is seen in the Son, Jesus Christ, who is the exact image of the Father. Therefore, when we pray to the Father, we can pray with the knowledge that our Father is just like Jesus. The Father and Jesus are One. And we come to Him on the basis of our relationship with Jesus, which gives us access to His presence. We can speak to God where all the resources of heaven are available.

Sometimes we may fail to realize just who our Father is, what He is capable of, and that He hears us when we pray. He is not only our Father but He is Almighty God, and because of this, there is a real reverence on our part toward Him. He is our Father and we have a loving relationship with Him, but at the same time, we are humbled by His presence.

Hallowing His Name speaks of holiness and reverence toward a Holy God and serves as an act of worship. The Bible talks about coming into His presence with thanksgiving and entering into His courts with praise, honoring who He is. Worship is a good element to enter into prayer with God and acts as a springboard to acknowledge His attributes and what He has done in our lives. When we worship God before listing our needs, our perspective of who He is increases the confidence we have in prayer. We realize that He is capable of moving mountains to solve problems and that nothing is impossible for Him because He is unlimited.

The Jews had such high respect for the name of God they felt their lips were unworthy to utter His name. Their minds were unworthy to even think the name of God. Therefore, when the scribes would copy the Scriptures and came across the name of God, they would omit the vowels: YHWH (Yahweh). Prior to inscribing His name, the scribes revered God so much that they would go through a purification ceremony and each time they encountered YHWH in the Scriptures, whether once or fifty times, they would have to re-purify themselves before they could jot His name down in their manuscripts.

He is our Father in heaven but He is also the Almighty God! Therefore, we approach His throne with a sense of reverence and respect. Hallowed implies holiness and reverence given to the name of God.

GOD'S MANY NAMES & TITLES

Throughout the Old Testament, we find many different titles attributed to the name of God as He connects with humans (see information box). These titles in the Old Testament reveal God's character to His people. Jehovah means the becoming one; if we need peace, God becomes Jehovah Shalom; if we need provision,

---

⊢ GOD'S NAMES AND TITLES ⊢

Elohim- meaning God Creator, Mighty and Strong (Genesis 1:1)

El Shaddai- for God Almighty, The Mighty One of Jacob (Genesis 49:24, Psalm 132:2,5) speaks to God's ultimate power over all;

Adoni- (Genesis 15:2; Judges 6:15) and Jehovah reference His proper name "Lord"used in place of YWHW; (Note: In the Old Testament YHWH is used in God's dealings with His people while Adonai is used with Gentiles;

Jehovah- Yahweh or LORD (translated in English Bibles with all capitals to distinguish from Lord (Adonai) – the revelation of God revealing Himself to Moses as "I Am That I Am" (Exodus 3:14); this name specifies an immediacy, a presence. Yahweh is present, accessible, near to those who call on Him for deliverance (Psalm 107:13), forgiveness (Psalm 25:11), and guidance (Psalm 31:3);

Jehovah Jireh- means The Lord Will Provide (Genesis 22:14), the name memorialized by Abraham when God provided the ram to be sacrificed in place of Isaac. God provides for our needs as well;

Jehovah Rapha- The Lord Who Heals (Exodus 15:26) "I am Jehovah who heals you" both in body and soul. In body by preserving from and curing diseases, and I soul by pardoning iniquities;

Jehovah Nissi- The Lord Our Banner (Exodus 17:15) where banner is understood to be a rallying place and commemorates the desert victory over the Amalekites

Jehovah M'kaddesh- The Lord Who Sanctifies or Makes Holy; (Jeremiah 23:6; 33:16; Leviticus 20:8; Ezekiel 37:28) God clarifies that He alone, not the law, can cleanse His people and make them holy

Jehovah Shalom- The Lord Our Peace (Judges 6:24) the name given by Gideon to the altar he built after the Angel of the Lord gave assurance he would not die after seeing Him

Jehovah Elohim- The Lord Our God (Genesis 2:4; Psalm 59:5) combination of God's unique name YHWH and the generic "Lord" signifying He is Lord of Lords

Jehovah Tsidkenu- The Lord Who Is Our Righteousness (Jeremiah 33:16) as Jehovah M'Kaddesh God alone provides righteousness ultimately in the person of His Son Jesus Christ who became sin for us "that we might become the righteousness of God in Him (2 Corinthians 5:21)

Jehovah Rohi- The Lord Our Shepherd (Psalm 23:1) after David pondered his relationship as a shepherd to his sheep he realized God's relationship to him and declared, "Yahweh-Rohi is my Shepherd. I shall not want"

Jehovah Shammah- The Lord Is There (Ezekiel 48:35) the name ascribed to Jerusalem and the Temple to indicate that the once departed glory of the Lord (Ezekiel 8-11) had returned (Ezekiel 44:1-4)

Jehovah Sabaoth- The Lord of Hosts (Isaiah 1:24; Psalm 46:7) Hosts means hordes of angels and men. He is Lord of the host of heaven and of the inhabitants of earth, of Jews and Gentiles, rich and poor, master and slave. This name is expressive of the majesty, power and authority of God and shows He is able to accomplish what he determines to do

El Elyon- The Most High God (Deuteronomy 26:19) derived from the Hebrew root for "go up" or "ascend" with the implication of the highest. El Elyon denotes exaltation and speaks of absolute right to lordship

El Roi- The God of the Seeing (Genesis 16:13), ascribed to God by Hagar in her moment of peril when she was alone and desperate in the wilderness after Sarah drove her away (Genesis 16:1-14). Hagar met the Angel of the Lord and realized she had seen God Himself as a theophany. El Roi saw her in distress and testified He is God who lives and sees all

El Olam- Everlasting God (Psalm 90:1-3) God's nature is without beginning or end, free from all constraints of time, and He contains within Himself the very cause of time itself: "From everlasting to everlasting, You are God"

El Gibhor- The Mighty God (Isaiah 9:6) describes the Messiah, Christ Jesus, in this prophetic portion of Scripture. As a powerful, mighty warrior, the Messiah, the Mighty God will accomplish the destruction of God's enemies and rule with a rod of iron (Revelation 19:15). (Source: Blue Letter Bible)

He becomes Jehovah Jireh, the God who provides; if we need healing, He is the God who heals. The Lord is all and in all and He is everything to us.

Therefore, we pray, "Our Father in heaven, hallowed be Thy Name." As we begin to consider the names of God describing His person (who He is), we cannot help revering and worshipping His name. Before we offer any personal requests, we recognize and revere His awesome power! We stand in awe of our God's majesty and splendor and we worship Him for who He is. Because our God is unlimited, this increases our confidence in prayer. Impossible is not in His vocabulary! "And those who know Your name will put their trust in You; For You, Lord, have not forsaken those who seek You" (Psalm 9:10). We move now in this model for prayer from *God's person* to *God's plan*.

VERSE 10: GOD'S PURPOSE

God in His person is our Father. His name is to be revered. Prayer begins with relationship—that's essential—and moves from recognition to worship of the Lord. Worship then moves into God's purpose. "Your kingdom come, Your will be done on earth as it is in heaven" (Matthew 6:10).

True prayer isn't overcoming God's reluctance but rather laying hold of His willingness. We need to align our will with His purpose because the foundation of prayer is for God to accomplish His will in our lives. When Mary received word that she was going to give birth to the Messiah, an angel revealed God's will to her of this marvelous news. The angel also revealed to her that there would be no end of His kingdom (Luke 6:33). As we petition the Lord for His kingdom to come, in one sense we are asking God to set up His kingdom personally in our lives so He can sit on the throne of our hearts. *Lord, you have the rightful place on the throne of my heart. I'm part of Your kingdom and You are my King. Be manifest in my life. Let the aspects of Your kingdom be seen.*

We don't live for this present kingdom. So, when we pray for God's kingdom to reign in our hearts and long for His kingdom to come, our prayer becomes global. The Bible tells us that God is eventually going to set up His kingdom here. When Daniel interpreted Nebuchadnezzar's dream about the kingdoms of the world, he spoke of a statue that represented the governing powers of the world and how one day, God's eternal kingdom would replace all other governments (Daniel 2:44-45).

Jesus *is* going to reign here on the earth forever and ever. He is going to set up His kingdom and there will no longer be any kingdoms of man under the sway of the devil, the prince of the power of the air who brings death and darkness, and who has blinded the eyes of so many. The devil has a kingdom of darkness but one day it will come to an end. We are praying for a kingdom of light and righteousness when we say, "Your kingdom come, Your will be done on earth as it is in heaven."

Creation also anticipates and longs for God's kingdom to reign. Paul writes in Romans: "For the earnest expectation of the creation eagerly waits for the revealing of the sons of God. For the creation was subjected to futility, not willingly, but because of Him who subjected *it* in hope; because the creation itself also will be delivered from the bondage of corruption into the glorious liberty of the children of God. For we know that the whole creation groans and labors with birth pangs together until now" (Romans 8:19-22). God's people and God's creation cry out for His kingdom! We anticipate His perfect will to be done on the earth as it is in heaven!

VERSES 11-13: PERSONAL PETITIONS FOR GOD'S PROVISION

In this model from Jesus on prayer, we began with the Lord, but now we move to our personal petitions with, "Give us this day our daily bread (v. 11)." Earlier, we learned the Lord knows our needs before we even ask, yet as we depend on our Provider, we present our needs to Him, and He is faithful to provide daily.

When the nation of Israel was making their way through the wilderness in the Book of Exodus, every single day the Lord provided manna. Daily bread from heaven fell to the ground so they wouldn't starve on their way to the Promised Land. God is faithful to provide what we need. He takes care of us. The psalmist wrote, "The Lord is my shepherd; I shall not want" (Psalm 23:1), and looking back says, "I have been young, and now am old, yet I have not seen the righteous forsaken, nor his descendants begging bread" (Psalm 37:25).

We are exhorted to trust God in all things: "Do not be anxious about anything, but in everything by prayer and supplication with thanksgiving let your requests be made known to God. And the peace of God, which surpasses all understanding, will guard your hearts and your minds in Christ Jesus" (Philippians 4:6-7 ESV). Paul goes on to say, in the same chapter, "And my God shall supply all your need according to His riches in glory by Christ Jesus" (v. 19).

GOD'S PARDON

Next, we move from God's daily provision to His pardon. "And forgive us our debts, as we forgive our debtors" (Matthew 6:12). The word debt in Scripture is one of the words used to denote sin. When Jesus went to the cross, He died for all our sins. We had a debt that we could not pay. He paid the debt that He did not owe. He completed the work. When He died on the cross, He said, "It is finished," translated, paid in full. The debt of humanity because of sin was paid in full by Christ through His own blood!

Though our sins have been forgiven—past, present, and future—we still sin. Whether inconsistent with the Lord in thought, action, word or deed, we can confess our sins to the Lord and repent, and He will forgive us. The Bible says, "If we confess our sins, He is faithful and just to forgive us our sins and to cleanse us from all unrighteousness" (1 John 1:9).

In addition to asking the Lord for forgiveness, we are instructed to forgive those who have wronged us. We are never more like Jesus than when we are forgiving, or as C. S. Lewis said, "To be a Christian means to forgive the inexcusable because God has forgiven the inexcusable in you."

GOD'S PROTECTION

Then there is the prayer for God's protection. Matthew 6:13 says, "And do not lead us into temptation, but deliver us from the evil one." This prayer is prayed from a heart knowing its own tendency to stray, to wander, to become tripped up by the flesh, and to ask for God's help to overcome temptations. It's a prayer from the heart of someone who knows there is a devil who goes about looking for someone to devour. They are well aware of the evil one and that we are in a spiritual battle. Thus, they look to the Lord for the power to overcome temptation.

It is not a sin to be tempted. Everybody is tempted, but it is a sin to give in to temptation, to pursue it, or to run after and embrace it. The Lord does not lead us into evil or temptation. As a Christian, the Lord allows us to be tested. It's been said faith that cannot be tested cannot be trusted. "My brethren, count it all joy when you fall into various trials, knowing that the testing of your faith produces patience. But let patience have its perfect work, that you may be perfect and complete, lacking nothing" (James 1:2-4). Trials are beneficial to develop our character in Christ, but while the devil seeks to bring us into temptation during a trial, Jesus seeks to direct us away from evil.

> "Blessed is the man who remains steadfast under trial, for when he has stood the test he will receive the crown of life, which God has promised to those who love him. Let no one say when he is tempted, 'I am being tempted by God,' for God cannot be tempted with evil, and he himself tempts no one. But each person is tempted when he is lured and

enticed by his own desire. Then desire when it has conceived gives birth to sin, and sin when it is fully grown brings forth death." James 1:12-15 (ESV)

The Bible tells us the Lord makes a way for us to escape temptation. "No temptation has overtaken you except such as is common to man; but God is faithful, who will not allow you to be tempted beyond what you are able, but with the temptation will also make the way of escape, that you may be able to bear it" (1 Corinthians 10:13). God always provides exits.

GOD'S POWER

How do we overcome temptation? The Bible encourages us to hide God's Word in our hearts that we might not sin against Him (Psalm 119:11). John wrote, "I have written to you, young men, because you are strong, and the word of God abides in you, and you have overcome the wicked one" (1 John 2:14).

Furthermore, the Word of God is the one offensive weapon at our disposal. When Jesus was confronted by Satan, He quoted Scripture, "Then Jesus was led up by the Spirit into the wilderness to be tempted by the devil. And after fasting forty days and forty nights, he was hungry. And the tempter came and said to him, "If you are the Son of God, command these stones to become loaves of bread." But he answered, "It is written, 'Man shall not live by bread alone, but by every word that comes from the mouth of God'" (Matthew 4:1-4 ESV).

The Devil also quoted—*misquoted*—Scripture, taking God's Word out of context. "Then the devil took him to the holy city and set him on the pinnacle of the temple and said to him, "If you are the Son of God, throw yourself down, for it is written, 'He will command his angels concerning you,' and 'On their hands they will bear you up, lest you strike your foot against a stone.' Jesus said to him, "Again it is written, 'You shall not put the Lord your God to the test.'" (Matthew 4:5-7 ESV).

THE LORDS PRAYER TEACHES US TO PRAY

The Enemy has studied mankind forever and knows our weak points, is keen on how he attacks different individuals, but Jesus always shows us there is a way out of temptation. We also pray for God's power as in Matthew 6:13, "For Yours is the kingdom and the power and the glory forever. Amen."

"The Lord's Prayer" begins with worship—*Hallowed be Your name*—that reveals God's plan and is followed by our petitions in-between and ends in worship. Before moving on from the topic of prayer, Jesus adds an important element: "Forgive us our debts, as we forgive our debtors" (Matthew 6:12).

13

FORGIVENESS

Jesus further stresses the importance of forgiveness, which goes hand-in-hand with His model prayer. "For if you forgive men their trespasses, your heavenly Father will also forgive you. But if you do not forgive men their trespasses, neither will your Father forgive your trespasses" (Matthew 6:14-15).

n light of the fact we are undeserving of God's forgiveness yet have been forgiven, we, in turn, are to forgive others. In the Book of Matthew, Jesus sheds light on how to confront a brother who has offended another and goes through a step-by-step process toward reconcilement. After Jesus gives this lesson, Peter comes to Jesus with a question. "Then Peter came to Him and said, 'Lord, how often shall my brother sin against me, and I forgive him? Up to seven times?' Jesus said to him, 'I do not say to you, up to seven times, but up to seventy times seven'" (Matthew 18:21-22 ESV).

Peter's question was significant because he wanted to know if forgiveness had limits. The religious leaders of Peter's day taught that a person was only required to forgive another person three times. This requirement was like the "three strikes you're out" law. But Peter thought his question was generous and more forgiving than most.

The religious leaders instated whoever begs forgiveness of a neighbor must not exceed the request more than three times. If a man commits an offense one to three times, they could receive forgiveness, but a fourth time was unforgivable. So, Jesus' response—one should not keep track—to Peter's question came as a shock! The Lord's forgiveness toward us is unlimited. Jesus said not to keep a record of wrongs and illustrated this lesson in a parable.

AN INSURMOUNTABLE DEBT WAS DUE

"Therefore the kingdom of heaven is like a certain king who wanted to settle accounts with his servants. And when he had begun to settle accounts, one was brought to him who owed him ten thousand talents" (Matthew 18:23-24 ESV).

THE PENALTY FOR INDEBTEDNESS

In modern terms, 10,000 talents are equivalent to an amount of money an ordinary citizen would not be able to pay back in a lifetime, plus, in this case, the debtor had added a penalty to the debt. "But as he was not able to pay, his master commanded that he be sold, with his wife and children and all that he had, and that payment be made" (Matthew 18:25 ESV).

PLEADING FOR FORGIVENESS

"The servant therefore fell down before him, saying, 'Master, have patience with me, and I will pay you all'" (Matthew 18:26 ESV).

FORGIVEN

"And out of pity for him, the master of that servant released him and forgave him the debt" (Matthew 18:27 ESV). The master completely forgave the debt, and the servant was free to go. Moments ago, he had no way to save himself or his family from a lifetime of servitude, but unmerited favor gave him a fresh start. However, this was not the end of the story.

The master did not offer the indebted man a payment plan but completely forgave him the debt and erased the balance on the books. One moment he was condemned to a life of slavery, losing everything, including his family, and the next moment, he was shown mercy, compassion, and forgiveness. The master cleared all of his debt, exercising amazing grace and undeserved mercy toward the man. One would think this man would be the happiest man on earth! The most grateful, compassionate, and merciful person on the planet!

UNMERCIFUL SERVANT

"But when that same servant went out, he found one of his fellow servants who owed him a hundred denarii, and seizing him, he began to choke him, saying, 'Pay what you owe.' So his fellow servant fell down and pleaded with him, 'Have patience with me, and I will pay you.' He refused and went and put him in prison until he should pay the debt" (Matthew 18:28-30 ESV).

ACTIONS REPORTED & HELD ACCOUNTABLE

"When his fellow servants saw what had taken place, they were greatly distressed, and they went and reported to their master all that had taken place. Then his master summoned him and said to him, 'You wicked servant! I forgave you all that debt because you pleaded with me. And should not you have had mercy on your fellow servant, as I had mercy on you?' And in anger his master delivered him to the jailers, until he should pay all his debt" (Matthew 18:31-34 ESV).

GOD'S JUDGMENT ON UNFORGIVENESS

"So also my heavenly Father will do to every one of you, if you do not forgive your brother from your heart" (Matthew 18:35 ESV).

When we look at this parable, we think, how could someone do that? How could they choke somebody out having been forgiven? We might say, that is ridiculous behavior, but let's apply this parable to ourselves.

The man in the story who owed the impossible debt represents us, lost in our sins. We owe a debt we can never pay. There are not enough righteous deeds, church attendances, tithings, or serving opportunities to pay the debt for our sins. There is no way out of eternal separation from God under the penalty of sin. Only by God's grace are we made aware of salvation in Christ and when we ask for God's forgiveness, He is not obligated to forgive us, redeem us, or pay our debt; yet, He moves with compassion. He paid our debt on the cross to forgive us. Now, we represent Jesus who forgave us.

This parable also reveals that we can never compare the debt we owe to any other debt someone else may owe us. Notice the size of the servant's debt. A denarius is nothing compared to ten thousand talents! The equivalent in today's market is about ten dollars versus ten million dollars. Therefore, this parable seems to imply, since we have been forgiven so great a debt, it is unreasonable and inconsistent for us not to forgive others.

We have been forgiven forever by God for immeasurable sin and, therefore, we are justified by faith as if our debt had never existed. From heaven's perspective, once the blood of Christ applied to our lives, we are completely forgiven, as though our "sin" debt never happened.

GOD'S DESIRE TO FORGIVE

As Christians, what is expected of us when people wrong us? What if someone says an unkind word to us? Slights or disrespects us in some way? Our response should be to extend that same forgiveness to others. People need forgiveness, and God desires to give forgiveness to others. "For You, Lord, are good, and ready to forgive, and abundant in mercy to all those who call upon You" (Psalm 86:5).

GOD IS THE SOURCE OF FORGIVENESS

God is ready to forgive, and He is also the source of forgiveness. The psalmist writes, "If You, Lord, should mark iniquities, O Lord, who could stand? But there is forgiveness with You, that You may be feared" (Psalm 130:3-4).

GOD HAS PROVIDED THE WAY TO FORGIVENESS

God desires to forgive, and He has provided a way for us to be forgiven. "In Him we have redemption through His blood, the forgiveness of sins, according to the riches of His grace which He made to abound toward us in all wisdom and prudence, having made known to us the mystery of His will, according to His good pleasure which He purposed in Himself, that in the dispensation of the fullness of the times He might gather together in one all things in Christ, both which are in heaven and which are on earth—in Him" (Ephesians 1:7-10).

THE EXTENT OF GOD'S FORGIVENESS

How far does God's forgiveness go? The Bible tells us, "And you, being dead in your trespasses and the uncircumcision of your flesh, He has made alive together with Him, having forgiven you all trespasses, having wiped out the handwriting of requirements that was against us, which was contrary to us. And He has taken it out of the way, having nailed it to the cross. Having disarmed principalities and powers, He made a public spectacle of them, triumphing over them in it" (Colossians 2:13-15).

The Lord's forgiveness provides freedom, joy, abundant life, and hope for eternity, among others. After David had sinned so horribly against the Lord and received God's forgiveness, he expressed his gratitude in Psalm 32, often titled *The Joy of Forgiveness*. David said, "Blessed is he whose transgression is forgiven, whose sin is covered.

Blessed is the man to whom the Lord does not impute iniquity, and in whose spirit there is no deceit" (vv. 1-2).

HIS EXAMPLE OF FORGIVENESS

God demonstrated His example of forgiveness for us. He spared no expense to provide that forgiveness, and now He calls us to forgive others, as well. The person who truly understands what forgiveness means is the one who will forgive.

OUR NEED TO FORGIVE OTHERS

However, forgiveness does not come easy for some. We don't mind asking the Lord for forgiveness for ourselves, but when it comes to others, forgiveness may be difficult. And God forbid if a person who has offended us does not ask us to forgive them. Be that as it may, God wants us to forgive.

Forgiving others does not give us the right to earn forgiveness from God, but forgiving others is significant because of what God has done for us to provide forgiveness. Forgiveness is not a suggestion. In fact, in Ephesians 4:32, we see that forgiveness is a command. "And be kind to one another, tenderhearted, forgiving one another, even as God in Christ forgave you." The Bible also tells us: "Therefore, as the elect of God, holy and beloved, put on tender mercies, kindness, humility, meekness, longsuffering; bearing with one another, and forgiving one another, if anyone has a complaint against another; even as Christ forgave you, so you also must do" (Colossians 3:12-13).

UNFORGIVENESS IMPRISONS

Unforgiveness can imprison us with bitterness, which entangles us with rotten fruit. Holding a grudge against another produces hostility. We may think withholding forgiveness from others affects them in a punishing way but the Bible says, "Strive for peace with everyone, and for the holiness without which no one will see the Lord. See to it that no one fails to obtain the grace of God; that no "root of bitterness" springs up and causes trouble, and by it many become defiled;" (Hebrews 12:14-15 ESV).

This paraphrase is attributed to Christian author and theology professor, Lewis B. Smedes: "When we genuinely forgive we set a prisoner free, and we discover that the prisoner we set free is us."

In light of God's command for us to forgive others, we may not always have the chance to sit down and reconcile with a person. Sometimes, a situation may be unsafe, or we may not have the option to make amends in person. Perhaps someone died or moved away. Nonetheless, God has made it clear we need to seek forgiveness. In these situations, we can extend forgiveness from our hearts. "Repay no one evil for evil. Have regard for good things in the sight of all men. If it is possible, as much as depends on you, live peaceably with all men" (Romans 12:17-18).

There are people in our lives the Lord calls us to forgive. If we don't forgive them, we are held in their vise grip and remain bound to those we cannot forgive.

EXAMPLES OF GOD'S POWER OF FORGIVENESS

Joseph is an excellent example of the power of forgiveness. His brothers wrecked his life by selling him into slavery. But when the tables turned, and Joseph became the second most powerful ruler in the world with the opportunity to get even, he chose to forgive his brothers.

"Joseph said to them, 'Do not be afraid, for am I in the place of God? But as for you, you meant evil against me; but God meant it for good, in order to bring it about as it is this day, to save many people alive. Now, therefore, do not be afraid; I will provide for you and your little ones.' And he comforted them and spoke kindly to them" (Genesis 50:19-21).

What about Stephen? Stephen, a dynamic deacon who served in the early church, gave one powerful sermon. He retraced the history of Israel and how the leaders forsook the Lord, ultimately rejecting Christ as Messiah. The religious leaders were cut to the heart by Stephen's sermon. They confronted this servant of God by picking up stones to kill him. While they were in the process of stoning Stephen to death, he pleaded with God, "Father, don't charge them with this sin," after which he was ushered into the presence of God.

Jesus is the greatest of all examples of the power of forgiveness. While hanging from the cross to pay the penalty of sin for the world, men cursed Him to His face, belittling Him and spitting at Him, telling Him to come down from the cross and save Himself. But had He saved Himself, He would not have been able to save us. His response to the crowd, "Father, forgive them, for they know not what they do," wasn't just for those standing at the foot of the cross at Golgotha. He was addressing all of humanity. God has forgiven us, and the Lord calls us to forgive others. As Jesus indicates in His Word, forgiveness has a tremendous impact on our personal prayer life. We are never more like Christ than when we forgive others.

14

FASTING

"Moreover, when you fast, do not be like the hypocrites, with a sad countenance. For they disfigure their faces that they may appear to men to be fasting. Assuredly, I say to you, they have their reward. But you, when you fast, anoint your head and wash your face, so that you do not appear to men to be fasting, but to your Father who is in the secret place; and your Father who sees in secret will reward you openly" (Matthew 6:16-18).

Fasting is another area where the disciples needed a guideline. Fasting is used some thirty times in the New Testament, and though the simplest form of fasting is abstinence from food, fasting is often associated with prayer and self-denial. Notice that Jesus said when you fast, not if you fast.

As Jesus shares on the subject of fasting, as in the other practices, the word "when," which implicates that fasting, like praying and giving, was part of the spiritual life of the disciples. However, for many fasting is more of an afterthought in our walk with the Lord.

Among Christians today, sacrificial giving and intercessory prayer is a more common practice than fasting. But reading through the Scriptures, we find various occasions when fasting was applied.

In 2 Samuel 12, King David resorted to fasting. The king had succumbed to temptation and sinned with Bathsheba, who gave birth to a son. The boy became sick, and David pleaded with the Lord for the recovery of the child, praying and fasting. He elaborated on the purpose of the fast: "I humbled myself with fasting, and my prayer would return to my own heart" (Psalm 35:13).

As the Moabites and Ammonites joined forces to destroy the southern kingdom of Judah, King Jehoshaphat cried out to the Lord in prayer and called for a fast that the people would seek help from God in times of distress. "And Jehoshaphat feared, and set himself to seek the Lord, and proclaimed a fast throughout all Judah. So Judah gathered together to ask help from the Lord; and from all the cities of Judah, they came to seek the Lord" (2 Chronicles 20:3-4).

The Book of Esther details the response of the Jewish people and how they petitioned the Lord for help in the wake of Haman's evil plan to exterminate them from the land (Esther 4:1-14). After Mordecai convinced Esther of Haman's plot, she called on the Jewish nation to join her in fasting and prayer before risking her life to plead to the king for her people. Then Esther told them to reply to Mordecai: "Go, gather all the Jews who are present in Shushan, and fast for me; neither eat nor drink for three days, night or day. My maids and I will fast likewise. And so I will go to the king, which is against the law; and if I perish, I perish!" (Esther 4:15-16).

Ezra tells of the release and return to Jerusalem of God's people who dwelt as captives in Babylon for seventy years. To seek favor of the Lord to rebuild their lives, they declared a fast.

When Jonah the prophet eventually landed in Nineveh, he declared because of their evil deeds, God was going to overthrow the entire city in forty days (Jonah 3:5-10).

In the New Testament, the Bible tells us that before Jesus entered His public ministry, He fasted for forty days in the wilderness where Satan tempted Him. After the fast, Jesus emerged victorious, empowered by the Spirit of God, and He began His fulltime ministry.

Paul, Barnabas, and other leaders gathered together in Antioch to seek the Lord for direction within the ministry. "As they ministered to the Lord and fasted, the Holy Spirit said, "Now separate to Me Barnabas and Saul for the work to which I have called them." Then, having fasted and prayed, and laid hands on them, they sent them away" (Acts 13:2-3). Later on, they repeated this practice with the elders: "So when they had appointed elders in every church and prayed with fasting, they commended them to the Lord in whom they had believed" (Acts 14:23).

God gave them specific direction as to their calling in life. The point here is that there are times when fasting is beneficial. To set aside a meal or meals to seek the Lord on a matter. Detaching ourselves from body appetites that so often control and dominate us. Our bodily appetites dominate our thinking and constantly grip us from meal to meal. As soon as our feet hit the ground in the morning, we make coffee and want something to eat. While packing lunch, we jot down a meal plan for dinner later.

Fasting helps us set aside the things of the flesh to grasp a heightened sensitivity to the things of the Spirit; to invest in the attribute of self-control, and further develop self-discipline over our flesh.

The purpose of fasting is not for people to notice us as spiritual and regimented and then somehow applaud us for our efforts. Jesus did not give His disciples specific, direct commandments concerning fasting, on how often or when to fast, or how many meals to abstain from and what fasting entailed. The New Testament does not give us a definitive guideline for fasting but seems to say fasting is up to our discretion as to when to abstain, and for how long. However, the Bible implies that this practice is part of a Christian's life.

While the disciples were with Jesus, they were criticized by the disciples of John the Baptist and the disciples of the Pharisees for not fasting as they did. John's disciples fasted habitually, and the Pharisees fasted regularly—two days a week—Tuesdays and Thursdays.

"Then the disciples of John came to Him, saying, 'Why do we and the Pharisees fast often, but Your disciples do not fast?' And Jesus said to them, 'Can the friends of the bridegroom mourn as long as the bridegroom is with them? But the days will come when the bridegroom will be taken away from them, and then they will fast'" (Matthew 9:14-15).

At that moment, Jesus said they were experiencing a celebration with the bridegroom, but when the bridegroom departs, the disciples will enter into a season of fasting. In Isaiah 58:3-9, the Bible indicates the purpose for fasting. The people were fasting for the wrong reasons with improper motivation, and they needed instruction on the proper motivation. Isaiah explains some benefits, such as the blessing of thinking about others and God's healing powers, as well as giving glory to the One who always has our back.

Fasting isn't a method to get the upper hand on God or to somehow obtain favor with the Lord. For example, if someone fasts for the sake of dieting, somehow this type of improper motivation will always weigh heavy. A person with the incentive to fast in this way could end up with visions of donuts dancing in their heads. Conversely, there are benefits to fasting and blessings that come with it, but it is vitally important we fast in a way that pleases God.

Notice, as it relates to fasting, Jesus tells His disciples what *not* to do. "Moreover, when you fast, do not be like the hypocrites, with a sad countenance, for they disfigure their faces that they may appear to men to be fasting. Assuredly, I say to you, they have their reward" (Matthew 6:16).

The first thing Jesus says is in reference to the hypocritical religious leaders. As Jesus indicates, they manifested their fasting with disheveled clothing, uncombed hair, and a long face to be seen by men. As the crowds observed these pious leaders with their pale and gaunt appearance, neglecting personal hygiene for the sake of being noticed as religious, the people would praise them for their dedication and commitment to fasting. As these religious leaders basked in the applause, the actual practice of fasting did nothing for them. Jesus said when we are rewarded of men, that is the only reward we will receive.

As for the hypocrites, they craved more than the desire to be seen by men. They wanted to be seen by men to please themselves and not to glorify God. Their behavior had people thinking too highly of them and had nothing to do with the Lord. The entire process was wrapped up in self and had to do with giving an impression for people to think they were serving God when, in reality, the opposite was true.

Though culturally acceptable and practiced regularly, Jesus told his disciples it didn't matter if everyone was practicing this type of fasting; it wasn't right to draw attention to oneself to take the glory and appear more spiritual. He contrasted such behavior in the next verses. "But you, when you fast, anoint your head and wash your face, so that you do not appear to men to be fasting, but to your Father who is in the secret place; and your Father who sees in secret will reward you openly" (Matthew 6:17-18).

Jesus instructed His disciples in this way so they would not indicate, even the slightest inference, in public that they were fasting. Instead, he taught them to seek the Lord in secret, and as they approached the Lord in this manner, they would be openly rewarded by Him. They were to fast in such a way that only God, and not men, could see and hear them.

The English cleric John Stott wrote, "The purpose of fasting is not to advertise ourselves but to discipline ourselves, not to gain a reputation for ourselves but to express our humility before God and our concern for others in need; if these purposes are fulfilled, it will be rewarded."

In light of this, the question we have to ask ourselves is: What do we desire? Temporary praise from people to see our good works and glorify us, or do we desire the reward of heaven?

Though some say fasting has become a lost art in the church with respect to teaching and practice, there are times when fasting and prayer are beneficial within the body. We can pray and fast for our nation or community and ask the Lord to intervene in other matters. Some may have major decisions to make, and it may be time to seek the Lord in fasting and prayer for direction. Others may have a lost loved one on their hearts. Whatever the concern, we can skip a meal and break away with the Lord to fast and pray for Him to intervene. In this way, we can make intercession for ourselves and others a priority in our lives.

TREASURES IN HEAVEN

"Do not lay up for yourselves treasures on earth, where moth and rust destroy and where thieves break in and steal; but lay up for yourselves treasures in heaven, where neither moth nor rust destroys and where thieves do not break in and steal. For where your treasure is, there your heart will be also" (Matthew 6:19-21).

E arlier, Jesus directed the disciples' attention to the private aspect of their lives, but now He draws their attention to public life and how the inner life, in their private devotions and prayer, directly impacts their public life. Jesus highlights how we spend our life in pairs: two treasures, earthly and heavenly; two ways of living, in light or darkness; and serving two masters: God or mammon.

First, He deals with the two treasures: "Do not lay up for yourselves treasures on earth." Again, Jesus is contrasting the righteousness accepted by God versus the false righteousness of the religious leaders, who the Bible tells us were lovers of money. In those days, great wealth signified great favor with God. Many were bound in materialism and used the ministry as a way to gain wealth. They would fleece the flock to indulge their flesh. When a rich, young ruler questioned Jesus on how to obtain eternal life, he was put off by the Lord's instruction to sell all he had to give to the poor and follow Him. The disciples, who were taught wealth meant God's hand was on their lives, were in for a surprise by what Jesus had to say about wealth finding favor with God (Matthew 19:23-26).

The problem with the rich, young ruler wasn't in how much he owned but that his material possessions owned him. In his case, all the treasures on earth could not save him spiritually, and he was bound by his wealth. The opiate for some is not the legalization or illegal use of drugs but the allure of amassing wealth and the addiction of earthly treasures. This situation can be likened to those who can't hear the message of the gospel because of various thorns (or distractions) in life. "Now he who received seed among the thorns is he who hears the word, and the cares of this world and the deceitfulness of riches choke the word, and he becomes unfruitful" (Matthew 13:22).

The thorns symbolize the deceitfulness of riches, the desire for more things, and the cares of this life. When a seed is planted amongst the cares of this world and deceitfulness of riches, these physical "thorns" in life intertwine, choking out God's spiritual message before it can grow into maturity. But money is not the root of all kinds of evil; the love of money is the root of all kinds of evil. "For the love of money is a root of all kinds of evil, for which some have strayed from the faith in their greediness, and pierced themselves through with many sorrows" (1 Timothy 6:10).

While it isn't wrong to have wealth, Job and Abraham were wealthy, the Bible warns us concerning setting one's heart on obtaining riches. The psalmist declares, "Do not trust in oppression, nor vainly hope in robbery; If riches increase, do not set your heart on them" (Psalm 62:10). We are not to get all wrapped up in hoping for riches to make a difference in our circumstances. Some say if they could only win the lottery, their whole life would change! All their problems would be instantly solved! In truth, many who walk away with a first prize ticket eventually end up right where they started. It's as though the money evaporated.

Jesus said it this way: "Take heed and beware of covetousness, for one's life does not consist in the abundance of the things he possesses" (Luke 12:15). In ancient times, wealth was often seen in the garments that a person wore. But Jesus warned that treasures on earth wouldn't last. He said if a thief doesn't steal our treasures, then a moth will. No matter what we wear or own, at some point, it will quit working in the way we want it to work, including our bodies. Everything we have is subject to decay except for eternal things.

It is easy to think our life is a reflection of what we own because we can only see the tangible treasures of this earth. But when we leave this earth, we will leave our possessions behind. It doesn't matter how big our houses are or how sweet our cars, or how awesome our earthly creations; none of these things have an eternal quality. "As he came from his mother's womb, naked shall he return, to go as he came; And he shall take nothing from his labor which he may carry away in his hand" (Ecclesiastes 5:15).

Ultimately, whatever God has entrusted to us belongs to Him, and as wise stewards of all that God provides, we can be thankful for our temporary blessings. Though we cannot envision eternal things at this moment, the Bible tells us we can store up treasures in heaven while here on earth. "Do not labor for the food which perishes, but for the food which endures to everlasting life, which the Son of Man will give you because God the Father has set His seal on Him" (John 6:27).

The Bible tells us: "Do not overwork to be rich; because of your own understanding, cease! Will you set your eyes on that which is not? For riches certainly make themselves wings; they fly away like an eagle toward heaven" (Proverbs 23:4-5). And the psalmist says, "Surely every man walks about like a shadow; surely they busy themselves in vain; he heaps up riches, and does not know who will gather them" (Psalm 39:6).

If we only live for temporary possessions, the potential remains to ensnare our hearts. If we don't consider this perspective, our hearts can become easily trapped by our treasures here on earth. Paul wrote to Timothy concerning the snare of riches. "But godliness with contentment is great gain, for we brought nothing into the world, and we cannot take anything out of the world. But if we have food and clothing, with these we will be content. But those who desire to be rich fall into temptation, into a snare, into many senseless and harmful desires that plunge people into ruin and destruction. For the love of money is a root of all kinds of evils. It is through this craving that some have wandered away from the faith and pierced themselves with many pangs" (1 Timothy 6:6-10 ESV).

Riches have the potential to drag us down and stunt our spiritual growth or to ensnare our hearts and make us its prisoner. But a shift in the heart from just laboring for temporary treasures to laboring in eternal treasures releases us from this sort of prison.

While we cannot take it with us, we can send it ahead or as Jesus said, "Lay up for yourselves treasures in heaven, where neither moth nor rust destroys and where thieves do not break in and steal. For where your treasure is, there your heart will be also" (Matthew 6:20-21). We lay up treasures in heaven by investing in the Kingdom of God with our lives, time, finances, or as a servant for the Lord. As we send our eternal investment ahead, nothing can touch this type of treasure as it is not subject to decay. Peter wrote: "Blessed be the God and Father of our Lord Jesus Christ! According to his great mercy, he has caused us to be born again to a living hope through the resurrection of Jesus Christ from the dead, to an inheritance that is imperishable, undefiled, and unfading, kept in heaven for you, who by God's power are being guarded through faith for a salvation ready to be revealed in the last time" (1 Peter 1:3-5 ESV).

We may or may not be blessed with an earthly inheritance in this world, but the Bible tells us, as children of God, we are joint-heirs of Christ and all that belongs to Him, He will share with us throughout eternity. Our Father in heaven is wealthier than anyone in this world.

He has given us all things to enjoy and at His right hand are pleasures forevermore.

Where is your heart today? Are you trying to hold on to things in the here and now or are you sending treasures ahead?

16

LIGHT VERSUS DARKNESS

"The lamp of the body is the eye. If therefore your eye is good, your whole body will be full of light. But if your eye is bad, your whole body will be full of darkness. If therefore the light that is in you is darkness, how great is that darkness!"
(Matthew 6:22-23).

There are two ways to live, but will we choose light over darkness? Every day we are bombarded with various temptations, and while some unexpected encounters are unavoidable, usually we are given a choice of how to filter such things. The eye is the lamp or lens of the body and acts as a filter and a gate to our hearts. What we take in through our eyes filters into the mind and travels to the heart. What we focus on, whether good or bad, makes its way to every part of our being and is manifested through our actions and lifestyle.

The point of the context is if our eyes focus solely upon a temptation, such as living for material things, then we can become blind and insensitive to spiritual concerns altogether. We can give into deception and confuse light with darkness and how great is that darkness. Jesus is saying to be discerning about what comes in through the eye. Decision-making begins with discernment. "Finally, brethren, whatever things are true, whatever things are noble, whatever things are just, whatever things are pure, whatever things are lovely, whatever things are of good report, if there is any virtue and if there is anything praiseworthy—meditate on these things. The things which you learned and received and heard and saw in me, these do, and the God of peace will be with you" (Philippians 4:8-9).

Job decided to be mindful of what he would not allow in his life. "I have made a covenant with my eyes; Why then should I look upon a young woman?" (Job 31:1). Paul wrote in 2 Corinthians 4:1-4 that we are a light to the world.

At present, the devil has blinded the minds of many whose focus is only on the things of the world. As Christians, it's important that the things with a direct impact on our minds are beneficial and that we set boundaries on how we should conduct our lives within God's Word. A traditional Sunday school song says it all: "Be careful little eyes what you see, be careful little ears what you hear … be careful little hands what you do, be careful little feet where you go … be careful little heart whom you trust, be careful little mind what you think … for the Father up above is looking down in love."

What are we taking in through our eyes? Is the focus of our vision measured by light or darkness?

17

TWO MASTERS

Jesus continues His sermon with, "No one can serve two masters; for either he will hate the one and love the other, or else he will be loyal to the one and despise the other. You cannot serve God and mammon" (Matthew 6:24).

N otice how emphatic He is: "No one can serve two masters ... you cannot serve God and mammon." Many have tried to serve two masters, but because of divided loyalty and divided interest, no one has been successful. In light of the context, Jesus is still talking about materialism. We can't serve God while worshipping the world.

Some Christians are dissatisfied with Jesus yet, at the same time, frustrated with the world. Others have enough of Jesus to fall short of contentment but enough of the world to block or stall the pursuit of Jesus with a whole heart. As Christians, it's hypocritical to think we can excuse our sin away by living a double life. It's a miserable existence to live our lives within these parameters. Our speech and decisions become dependent upon which crowd we are with at the moment.

In the Old Testament, the prophets would constantly call the people back from the high places. The people would be drawn into idolatry, making their lives unbearable with enemies oppressing them on every side. They would return to the Lord only to slide right back into the culture, repeating the cycle all over again.

The prophet Samuel pleaded with the people to forsake their idols and serve the Lord. (1 Samuel 7:3-4), but God didn't force them to put away the idols to serve Him; He gave them a choice. Did they want to be oppressed and crushed by the enemy, or did they want His protection? The decision of which master to serve was up to them. Did they want to live in fear and bondage, or did they desire deliverance from God?

Elijah came to all the people and asked them how long they were going to waver between two opinions. How long were they going to stand at a crossroads and straddle the fence? (1 Kings 18:20-21). In 2 Kings 17:33, an indictment came against the children of Israel; though they feared God, they still served idols.

Then in Zephaniah, the Lord made another indictment: "I will stretch out my hand against Judah, and against all the inhabitants of Jerusalem; and I will cut off from this place the remnant of Baal and the names of the idolatrous priests along with the priests, those who bow down on the roofs to the host of the heavens, those who bow down and swear to the Lord and yet swear by Milcom, those who have turned back from following the Lord, who do not seek the Lord or inquire of him" (Zephaniah 1:4-6 ESV).

There was a problem with the nation of Israel. They were divided, trying to serve two masters. Jesus said you cannot serve two masters because you will despise the one and be loyal to the other. Self-deception is one of the most frightening results of living a divided life with a divided heart. We may live one way on Friday evening and then "clean ourselves up" to attend church on Sunday, thinking this is good enough for the Lord. But, is this the type of relationship the Lord wants with us? Is this the type of relationship we would want with others? We all have a choice to make to serve one master. *Who do you want to serve?*

NO NEED TO WORRY

I n this portion of the "Sermon on the Mount," Jesus deals with the subject of worry. "Therefore I say to you, do not worry about your life, what you will eat or what you will drink; nor about your body, what you will put on. Is not life more than food and the body more than clothing? Look at the birds of the air, for they neither sow nor reap nor gather into barns; yet your heavenly Father feeds them. Are you not of more value than they? Which of you by worrying can add one cubit to his stature?"

"Therefore, I tell you, do not be anxious about your life, what you will eat or what you will drink, nor about your body, what you will put on. Is not life more than food, and the body more than clothing? Look at the birds of the air: they neither sow nor reap nor gather into barns, and yet your heavenly Father feeds them. Are you not of more value than they? And which of you by being anxious can add a single hour to his span of life?

And why are you anxious about clothing? Consider the lilies of the field, how they grow: they neither toil nor spin, yet I tell you, even Solomon in all his glory was not arrayed like one of these. But if God so clothes the grass of the field, which today is alive and tomorrow is thrown into the oven, will he not much more clothe you, O you of little faith? Therefore, do not be anxious, saying, 'What shall we eat?' or 'What shall we drink?' or 'What shall we wear?' For the Gentiles seek after all these things, and your heavenly Father knows that you need them all. But seek first the kingdom of God and his righteousness, and all these things will be added to you. Therefore, do not be anxious about tomorrow, for tomorrow will be anxious for itself. Sufficient for the day is its own trouble." (Matthew 6:25-34 ESV).

As we look at our world, we see many troubling situations, such as the increase of violence upon the earth in the form of global terrorism, as never before. We read of civil and tribal wars around the world and hear of countries striving to gain chemical, nuclear, and biological weapons. We see racial tensions escalating in different parts of the country and a backlash of response in the form of riots and hatred. We see an increase in natural disasters through fires, floods, and earthquakes, such as the quake that affected two million people in Indonesia.

We read of new diseases surfacing that doctors cannot find a cure for and we observe an agenda to do away with marriage, as God intended. We see the ongoing battle to protect the life of the unborn, legalization of marijuana, and the devastating consequences that will follow. Our school systems continue to rewrite our history books and remove the foundation of Biblical principles that established the country. In its place, we find sexually perverse curriculum placed before our children in public schools, while educators tell them God does not exist. We see an increased addiction to pornography at our fingertips, leadership faltering at the highest level, and a nation divided on society-altering issues. The rise of false religious systems is leading people astray. We even see churches turning away from the Bible, embracing false doctrines, and accepting worldly practices in the name of tolerant love. All of these things and more can cause great turmoil and anxiety.

Our medical doctors are doing their best to identify and diagnose problems that cause worry and anxiety, fear, and depression. Anxiety disorders are the most common mental illness in the United States and affect some 40 million adults from age 18 and older. Year-over-year, 18.1 percent of the population is affected. Depression is the leading cause of disability worldwide. In developing countries, nearly 75 percent of those with mental disorders remain untreated with some one million people taking their lives each year. Also, according to the World Health Organization, on a global scale, an estimated 300 million people suffer from anxiety—the most common mental disorder worldwide—with specific phobias, major depressive disorders, and with social phobias at the top of the list. People with anxiety disorders—from PTSD to social anxieties to panic attacks and more—are three to five times more likely to go to the doctor and six times more likely to be hospitalized for psychiatric disorders than those who do not suffer from these disorders.

According to the Economic Burden of Anxiety Disorders, a study commissioned by the ADAA (Anxiety and Depression Association of America), and based on data gathered by the association, and published in the Journal of Clinical Psychiatry, anxiety disorders cost the United States more than $42 billion a year. This amount is almost one-third of the annual $148 billion total mental health bill with more than $22.84 billion associated with those costs from the repeated use of health care services for anxiety disorders where people seek relief for symptoms of physical illness. Some 65 percent of North Americans take prescription medications daily, and 43 percent take mood-altering prescriptions regularly.

More recent studies reveal a steady increase in anxiety disorders, citing some 46.6 million (in 2017) adults in America experiencing mental health issues in a given year. The National Alliance on Mental Illness reports that serious mental illness costs America $193 billion in lost earnings every year.

These statistics point to the fact that we are anxious, worried, depressed, and fearful people. Sometimes we may try to make light of these facts with slogans on stickers, tee-shirts, or mugs that attempt to help us cope. Such sayings include: "Keep calm and carry on," "Keep calm and eat a banana," "Keep calm and drink coffee," or "Keep calm and hug a panda." While clever anecdotes may sell products, these won't help anyone in a real crisis or while dealing with real issues, like we see today.

In the world, a great many things can trouble us but we can turn to our Great Physician, Jesus Christ, to receive His diagnosis for any problem we may face, and we can take His living Word as a prescription for our anxious minds.

Jesus' message about worry to His disciples reveals how they should conduct their lives within this world. Worry is defined as mental anxiety or stress, to feel, or cause to feel, troubled over actual or potential difficulties. Worry suggests fretting over matters that may or may not be a real cause for the anxiety. The Greek word most commonly used within these verses—*merimnaó*—basically means "to be anxious or worried," but another definition means "to go to pieces, to be pulled in different directions." This gives us a picture that describes the experience of what it feels like to worry about matters in this world.

Worry occurs when people are so concerned about the problems of this world, they cannot think of anything else. Worry can become a crippling, all-consuming sense of uncertainty and fear. Jesus highlights some causes for worry. First, it is important to keep in mind the word "therefore." In Matthew 6:25, *therefore* takes us back to all the statements Jesus made previously. When looking back to the beginning of the "Sermon on the Mount," we see Jesus mentioned some dangers associated with misplaced attributions.

MISPLACED AFFECTIONS

Jesus covers the danger of misplaced affections: "Do not lay up for yourselves treasures on earth, where moth and rust destroy and where thieves break in and steal, but lay up for yourselves treasures in heaven, where neither moth nor rust destroys and where thieves do not break in and steal. For where your treasure is, there your heart will be also" (Matthew 6:19-21 ESV).

Earthly treasures are temporary and, ultimately, do not last; whereas, spiritual treasure sent ahead to heaven is eternal. Jesus exhorted His disciples to be careful and not merely lay up treasures on earth without making provision for eternity. If the disciples placed all of their affection and focus solely on temporary items, this would have the potential to cause them to worry.

A great example of this type of worry in the Old Testament is seen in the life of King Solomon, most likely the wealthiest person who ever lived. But as we read about his life, specifically in the Book of Ecclesiastes, we discover that having amassed much wealth and treasure, Solomon was so disturbed and anxious about having to leave his fortune to his "foolish" son that he declared, "Everything is vanity." He thought to himself, What a waste! I worked for all this, and I have to leave it to this kid! Ecclesiastes clearly records Solomon's overarching concerns and worries over his earthly treasures.

MISPLACED ATTENTION

Jesus also pointed to the importance of being careful of misplaced attention. "The eye is the lamp of the body. So, if your eye is healthy, your whole body will be full of light, but if your eye is bad, your whole body will be full of darkness. If then the light in you is darkness, how great is the darkness!" (Matthew 6:22-23 ESV).

The lamp Jesus refers to is the lens of the eye—what we look at and focus our attention on. Subject matter filters into our minds and makes its way to our hearts, which then translates into action. If we focus only on negative impressions, then we will be affected negatively. Conversely, if our attention fixates on positive, godly, and edifying impressions, that will impact us in a positive, godly way.

If our eyes fixate on evil, we will become greatly discouraged and troubled. If we feed on the constant newsfeeds of the day, we can become overburdened. Too much information heaped upon us without the filter of God's Word is impossible to process and can weigh us down, making us troubled and cynical about many things. The world cries out: Focus on this! This is what you should labor to obtain! This is what you should believe! Embrace this! We are bombarded nonstop from every direction, and depending upon our focus and attention, the onslaught can easily cause us to become overwhelmed.

When Jesus and His disciples made their way down to Bethany to visit Mary, Martha, and Lazarus, they showed up unannounced. Martha, the hostess, immediately went into action. She started cooking up a storm in the kitchen, probably banging pots and pans in a frenzy to provide food for the unexpected guests. Meanwhile, according to Luke's gospel, Mary fell into worship, fellowshipping with the Lord.

"But Martha was distracted with much serving. And she went up to him and said, 'Lord, do you not care that my sister has left me to serve alone? Tell her then to help me.' But the Lord answered her, 'Martha, Martha, you are anxious and troubled about many things, but one thing is necessary. Mary has chosen the good portion, which will not be taken away from her'" (Luke 10:40-42 ESV).

There was much more going on in Martha's life than what was going on in the kitchen. The fact she felt so overwhelmed indicates other stressful things going on in her life, causing her to react in this way. The impromptu visit just tipped the scale for a woman already upset. Jesus ministered to Martha by pointing to Mary.

We, too, can make the mistake of becoming worried and troubled about many things because of misplaced attention. If our focus is not on Jesus, our focus will be on everything else. If we don't take time to sit at His feet, life can overwhelm us, and this can cause us to question God's care and concern for us, like the disciples' response when they were in the midst of a storm. The storm was raging, but the disciples gave in to misplaced attention until they refocused on Jesus for the storm of such great concern to cease (Mark 4:36-41).

Peter is another example. The Bible tells us about Peter's misplaced attention when Jesus told him about his impending mortality. "Then Peter, turning around, saw the disciple whom Jesus loved [John] following ... Peter, seeing him, said to Jesus, 'But Lord, what about this man?' Jesus said to him, 'If I will that he remain till I come, what is that to you? You follow Me'" (John 21:20-22).

In other words, if we are distracted by others, misplaced attention can cause us considerable worry. Instead, we need to focus on the Lord and listen to what He has to say to us in His Word.

MISPLACED ALLEGIANCE

Another concern is misplaced allegiance. In Matthew 6:24, Jesus says, "No one can serve two masters; for either he will hate the one and love the other, or else he will be loyal to the one and despise the other. You cannot serve God and mammon."

Jesus is definitive on this subject. He is not saying, "You can try to serve two masters, give it a shot!" He's saying it is not possible to serve two masters! In context, Jesus emphasizes those with a divided heart are caught up in materialism. If a person tries to live in two worlds at the same time, it's going to create a stressful situation, and in the process, that person will become anxious. Whatever we set our affections and focus on impacts our mental and spiritual health. We can pinpoint our anxieties by questioning our loyalties.

THE BIBLE GIVES US SEVERAL REASONS why we are not to worry. In Matthew 6:25, we are told, "Therefore I say to you, do not worry about your life, what you will eat or what you will drink; nor about your body, what you will put on." The phrase "do not worry" literally means take no anxious thought. Jesus uses this phrase three times as a command. Some make the mistake that Jesus is saying we should not even think about worrying. But it is okay to think about something of concern to pray about it. He is also not saying we should not plan for a worrisome situation. Jesus is saying we should not become preoccupied with worry because this will cause anxiety.

Insofar as our bodily appetites go, again, we are bombarded with advertisements that cater to our bodies in the form of billboards, magazines, online popups, and on-air ads. What are we going to wear? Where are we going to eat? Where are we going on our next vacation? Jesus told the disciples not to be consumed by such thoughts. The Bible shows us how to combat our thoughts. "For the weapons of our warfare are not carnal but mighty in God for pulling down strongholds, casting down arguments and every high thing that exalts itself against the knowledge of God, bringing every thought into captivity to the obedience of Christ" (2 Corinthians 10:4-5).

When our flesh or our circumstances or the enemy suggests a thought or attempts to insight fear, our recourse is to take the matter back to Jesus to measure whether or not the matter at hand is worthy of our consideration. In Colossians, the apostle Paul said, "If then you have been raised with Christ, seek the things that are above, where Christ is, seated at the right hand of God. Set your minds on things that are above, not on things that are on earth. For you have died, and your life is hidden with Christ in God. When Christ who is your life appears, then you also will appear with him in glory" (Colossians 3:1-4 ESV).

First and foremost, Jesus commands us not to worry. When everything is fighting for the space in our brain, we can initiate a mental exercise to bring our thoughts from earthly matters to the eternal things of heaven and to focus on our purpose as Christians.

Life is more than materialism, and this gives us another reason not to worry over bodily concerns.

THERE IS SO MUCH MORE TO LIFE

Jesus asks a practical question that sparks our attention: "Is not life more than food and the body more than clothing?" In other words, there is much more to life than these basic concerns. Yet, we can see, touch, and taste tangible items making it seem difficult to think about eternal things we have never seen.

Paul's second letter to the Corinthians addresses the invisible things of God. "So we do not lose heart. Though our outer self is wasting away, our inner self is being renewed day by day. For this light momentary affliction is preparing for us an eternal weight of glory beyond all comparison, as we look not to the things that are seen but to the things that are unseen. For the things that are seen are transient, but the things that are unseen are eternal" (2 Corinthians 4:16-18 ESV).

Paul looked beyond the physical plane of our temporary existence toward eternity through the eyes of faith. Once we understand that life is worth more than materialism, there is no need to fret over temporary things.

JESUS POINTS TO NATURE AS AN EXAMPLE

Jesus draws attention to His creatures that do not worry about provision: "Look at the birds of the air, for they neither sow nor reap nor gather into barns; yet your heavenly Father feeds them. Are you not of more value than they?" (Matthew 6:26). More importantly, Jesus assures us that God loves us. He encourages the disciples to bird watch. Who provides for the birds? Do birds stress, pulling out their feathers, freaking out in search of food? The Bible tells us, "For since the creation of the world His invisible attributes are clearly seen, being understood by the things that are made, even His eternal power and Godhead" (Romans 1:20).

God's creation shows evidence of His provision; He designed creatures with instinct, the heavens declare His glory, and the firmament shows His handiwork. In creation, we see the faithfulness of God, even in providing for the least of His creatures. And if God provides for the least of His creatures, He is going to provide for His children. God provided salvation, purchasing us with His own blood. "Greater love has no one than this, than to lay down one's life for his friends" (John 15:13), and His perfect love casts out fear: "There is no fear in love; but perfect love casts out fear, because fear involves torment. But he who fears has not been made perfect in love. We love Him because He first loved us" (1 John 4:18-19).

WE ARE LOVED BY GOD

The Bible assures us God loves us and that He provides all things: "Behold what manner of love the Father has bestowed on us, that we should be called children of God!" (1 John 3:1); "What then shall we say to these things? If God is for us, who can be against us? He who did not spare His own Son, but delivered Him up for us all, how shall He not with Him also freely give us all things?" (Romans 8:31-32).

If the Lord loved us enough not to spare His own Son but allowed Him to be crucified, is He not going to take care of us? He settled the greatest problem of humanity—salvation—and is more than capable of provision for the greatest of His creatures. When in doubt of God's love, we need to look back at the cross, at the hands and feet pierced for us. Think about Him and consider Him. Why are we worried?

WORRY WON'T CHANGE ANYTHING

Jesus brings up another reason not to worry in Matthew 6:27, "Which of you by worrying can add one cubit to his stature?" Some commentators suggest that "one cubit" refers to one's height. Others indicate the cubit refers to a span of someone's life; either way, the point is worrying over a cubit of measurement won't change a thing! Worry doesn't alter the situation. Worry won't add inches to our height or years to a lifespan. Nobody ever lived longer by worrying, and in fact, worrying could shorten a lifespan.

How many people worry about involuntary breathing before they close their eyes at night? Will your heart keep beating as you sleep? Will the sun come up tomorrow? There are many things to worry about, but Jesus commands us to refocus our worries.

The Bible tells us, "Rest in the Lord, and wait patiently for Him; Do not fret because of him who prospers in his way, because of the man who brings wicked schemes to pass. Cease from anger, and forsake wrath; Do not fret—it only causes harm" (Psalm 37:7-8).

The cares of this life can choke out what God wants to do in our lives, and worry can hinder our spiritual growth. We need to bring Jesus in the midst of our cares for the strength and faith to cope. In Matthew 6:28-30, Jesus said, "Consider the lilies of the field, how they grow: they neither toil nor spin; and yet I say to you that even Solomon in all his glory was not arrayed like one of these. Now if God so clothes the grass of the field, which today is, and tomorrow is thrown into the oven, will He not much more clothe you, O you of little faith?"

Jesus compares the beauty of lilies to King Solomon, one of the most fashionable, resplendent kings in history. During springtime in Israel, an array of flowers spread across the fields and mountains like an artist's colorful canvas. Flora does not toil or spin its wheels. If the Lord allows these flowers to blossom and bloom, bringing a fragrant beauty to the earth, surely He will care for, clothe and provide for His children.

Some have the idea that Jesus brings blessings to us, that just like the flowers in the field, we don't need to assert any energy to make things happen. Throughout this passage, Jesus is not saying we should not work or seek out a job. Trusting God is not a license for laziness. The Bible says the person who doesn't work doesn't eat. As the Lord leads, we need to do our part, giving glory to God. "Trust in the Lord with all your heart, and lean not on your own understanding; In all your ways acknowledge Him, And He shall direct your paths" (Proverbs 3:5-6).

WORRY IS AN ENEMY TO FAITH

Another point as it relates to worrying is that worry is a great enemy to our faith. The Bible declares, "But without faith, it is impossible to please Him, for he who comes to God must believe that He is and that He is a rewarder of those who diligently seek Him," (Hebrews 11:6). Worry can never see what faith sees. Faith sees the unseen; faith believes and trusts in the promises of God while worry doubts His promises. Rather than taking hold of the above verse, worry finds all the reasons why that verse does not apply to everyone.

When Jesus called Peter out onto the water during a storm, as soon as Peter focused on the wind and waves in the sea, he began to sink. Peter then prayed for Jesus to save him and once they were back in the boat, Jesus comforted him that there was no reason ever to doubt that he could've continued to walk on water during the storm. At one time or another, we all take our eyes off the Lord during a storm. In so doing, we stop short of an accomplishment.

FAITH COMES BY HEARING

Attributed to George Müller, it's been said, "The beginning of anxiety is the end of faith, and the beginning of true faith is the end of anxiety." The Bible says, "Faith comes by hearing, and hearing by the Word of God" (Romans 10:17). We are told to stand by faith (Romans 11:20) and exhorted to believe in faith. We are saved by faith and walk by faith. 'For whatever is born of God overcomes the world. And this is the victory that has overcome the world—our faith' (1 John 5:4).

When we doubt the Lord, this can indicate we lack faith and trust in the Lord. Faith and worry are mutually exclusive. All of us face situations that cause us to worry. Given the right circumstance, we are prone to worry. It's a natural character flaw, but when this happens, we can consider the faithfulness of God.

After the Lord subdued Israel's enemies, Samuel the prophet commemorated what the Lord had done on their behalf. "Then Samuel took a stone and set it up between Mizpah and Shen, and called its name Ebenezer, saying, 'Thus far the Lord has helped us'" (1 Samuel 7:12).

As the nation of Israel crossed over the Jordan River, Joshua set up twelve stones, which represented the twelve tribes of Israel, in the middle of the Jordan. He commanded his men to stack twelve stones from the river after they crossed over as a memorial that God brought them across the river to get to the Promised Land. They first camped at Gilgal, which became a landmark for the Israelites, after a battle to remember God brought them across the Jordan River. He brings us across our "Jordan Rivers," too, but He doesn't leave us there. As Christians, Jesus Christ is our Gilgal.

Jesus told His disciples a parable about faith: "The kingdom of heaven is like a mustard seed, which a man took and sowed in his field, which indeed is the least of all the seeds; but when it is grown it is greater than the herbs and becomes a tree, so that the birds of the air come and nest in its branches" (Matthew 13:31-32); later, when they failed to cure a child of a demon, they again approached Jesus about faith, this time asking why they couldn't cure the child. "So Jesus said to them, 'Because of your unbelief; for assuredly, I say to you, if you have faith as a mustard seed, you will say to this mountain, 'Move from here to there,' and it will move; and nothing will be impossible for you'" (Matthew 17:20).

FIELD GUIDE FOR YOUR FAITH: Sermon on the Mount

Based on the fact that Jesus is faithful, we are not to worry. He loves us, and our life is worth more than materialism. God knows what we need. "Therefore, do not worry, saying, 'What shall we eat?' or 'What shall we drink?' or 'What shall we wear?' For after all these things the Gentiles seek. For your heavenly Father knows that you need all these things" (Matthew 6:31-32). When Jesus said, "For after all these things the Gentiles seek," he was referring to the mentality of the world.

GOD KNOWS WHAT WE NEED

The Bible says the Lord knows what His children need even before they ask. He may not grant a request because He is well aware of the truth that sometimes the things we think we need are really not what we need. "For after all these things the Gentiles seek. For your heavenly Father knows that you need all these things" (Matthew 6:32).

The world, preoccupied with bodily appetites, drives and pursues "needs" with passion. In his book, "The Message of the Sermon on the Mount" by John Stott, he wrote that in the vocabulary of Jesus "to seek" and "to be anxious" are interchangeable. "He is not talking so much about anxiety as about ambition. Now heathen ambition focuses on material necessities. But this cannot be right for Christians partly because your heavenly Father knows that you need them all, but mostly because these things are not an appropriate or worthy object for the Christian's quest. He must have something else, something higher, as the Supreme Good, which he will energetically seek."

Paul wrote to the church in Philippi, "And my God shall supply all your need according to His riches in glory by Christ Jesus" (Philippians 4:19).

Then, why are we so troubled and anxious? If we enter each day or days or weeks and months-on-end without first seeking God, our spiritual needs will suffer, and this leads to worry.

152

THE CURE FOR WORRY

Jesus gave us the cure for worry, and the antidote is to make a daily choice to prioritize God's kingdom and His righteousness by seeking Him first through prayer and His Word. This good news is found in the Bible. "But seek first the kingdom of God and His righteousness, and all these things shall be added to you" (Matthew 6:33).

"Therefore, do not worry about tomorrow, for tomorrow will worry about its own things. Sufficient for the day is its own trouble" (Matthew 6:34). We can overcome anxiety if we make a habit of spending one moment at a time with Jesus. "Do not be anxious about anything, but in everything by prayer and supplication with thanksgiving let your requests be made known to God. And the peace of God, which surpasses all understanding, will guard your hearts and your minds in Christ Jesus" (Philippians 4:6-7 ESV).

Instead of giving in to anxiety, we can give in to prayer and God's promise of His peace, which surpasses our understanding and acts as a garrison of soldiers, will surround and guard us. Only Jesus can offer peace and rest in turmoil. "Come to Me, all you who labor and are heavy laden, and I will give you rest. Take My yoke upon you and learn from Me, for I am gentle and lowly in heart and you will find rest for your souls. For My yoke is easy, and My burden is light" (Matthew 11:28-30).

A fine line exists between anxiety and awareness, trusting or stressing, but if we take time to seek the Lord first, we will receive the assurance that He will supply all our needs.

19

JUDGING

"Judge not, that you be not judged. For with what judgment you judge, you will be judged; and with the measure you use, it will be measured back to you. And why do you look at the speck in your brother's eye, but do not consider the plank in your own eye? Or how can you say to your brother, 'Let me remove the speck from your eye'; and look, a plank is in your own eye? Hypocrite! First remove the plank from your own eye, and then you will see clearly to remove the speck from your brother's eye" (Matthew 7:1-5).

W e come to the final chapter of the "Sermon on the Mount." Found within this sermon, we have observed the consistent contrast between the Pharisaical self-righteousness of the religious leaders versus the righteousness God accepts. While the righteousness of the religious leaders, based on external practices of piety and demonstrated by righteous deeds through their outward performance to be seen by men, this flawed human attempt to appear righteous in the sight of God falls short of the standard of requirements. The only righteousness acceptable to God is the righteousness of Christ, which cannot be earned but only imputed to us through faith in His finished work on the cross on our behalf.

On the subject of judging one another, "Judge not, that you be not judged" is one of the most well known and misunderstood verses in the Bible. Within this context, it is essential to understand what Jesus meant by the word "judge" precisely.

Some use this verse ("Don't judge me!") as a response to justify certain behavior. However, usage of this passage in that way is out of the context of its true meaning. Jesus is not saying that, given any circumstance, it is wrong to pass unfavorable judgment on the conduct of others. In that vein, the Bible clearly instructs us to be discerning. 1 Thessalonians 5:21 tells us to test all things and hold fast to that which is good.

We must have an opinion to make a judgment call on right from wrong. The apostle writes, "Beloved, do not believe every spirit, but test the spirits, whether they are of God; because many false prophets have gone out into the world" (John 4:1).

In writing to the Corinthians, the apostle Paul exhorted them to test things and discern with wise judgment some of the troubling things transpiring in Corinth. The Corinthians were tolerating and embracing sin and suing one another in court, so Paul wrote the letter to find someone within the congregation godly and discerning enough to judge between those who were at odds. Paul was asking for someone in the church with good judgment to step up and help the people with issues. In that same epistle, Paul reminded the church that one day, they were going to judge angels (1 Corinthians 6:1-6).

Good judgment requires a balance. In this context, Jesus forbids hypocritical fault-finding attitudes or opinions. A readiness to find fault and pass the blame on others with minor issues that have no bearing on eternity or a person's walk with God. Passing hasty judgment on others is a far too common and unhealthy habit. Jesus condemns a mindset and attitude of consistently magnifying others' errors.

The very word "judge" that Jesus forbids refers to one who actively enjoys reporting the dirt they dig up about others. Such a person takes the role of a divine judge, a position that has already been filled by the Lord. We are not qualified to take this position; we cannot see the hearts of people. We do not know what is going on inside of a person, as Paul wrote in Romans 2:1-3; 12; 16.

Only the Lord knows what is in the heart of a person.

The Gospels record numerous times when the scribes and Pharisees practiced unmerciful condemnation of others. Mark 7:1-3 records an occasion when the religious leaders observed the disciples failing to wash their hands in a prescribed, traditional manner and deemed them unclean. The scribes and Pharisees wrongly misjudged the disciples from outward appearances, but Jesus said defilement comes from within a person and not from without. "Do you not perceive that whatever enters a man from outside cannot defile him, because it does not enter his heart but his stomach, and is eliminated, thus purifying all foods?" And He said, "What comes out of a man, that defiles a man" (Mark 7:19-20).

In one instance, the religious leaders falsely accused the disciples of harvesting wheat on the Sabbath when they were merely grazing stalks of grain, perhaps to subdue appetite. Another time, when Jesus healed a blind man on the Sabbath, the leaders unlawfully judged Him, saying He was working on the Sabbath. The Pharisees continuously practiced ill judgment against society.

Often, people who misjudge others are trying to prove they're right and everyone else is wrong. They elevate themselves as the standard measurement of proper behavior. *Krino* is the Greek word for "judge" and means "to separate, choose, select, or determine." When Jesus speaks of judging others' motives, he is not suggesting blind and undiscerning behavior but graciousness. The Bible says, "Therefore, let us not judge one another anymore but rather resolve this, not to put a stumbling block or a cause to fall in our brother's way" (Romans 14:13).

We may pass quick judgment on another person when we don't have all the information. A judgment call made on partial information is inaccurate. Proverbs 18 says, "He who answers a matter before he hears it, it is folly and shame to him;" (v. 13), and further along in that same chapter, "The first one to plead his cause seems right until his neighbor comes and examines him" (v. 17).

It's essential to get all the facts before attempting to make any kind of judgment call. Jesus gives us several reasons why we should not judge in a condemning way. First, the most obvious reason is that it is a command. Jesus said, "Judge not that you be not judged" (Matthew 7:1). True disciples of Jesus will seek to obey His precept, but those who judge others in this regard are actually breaking a command of the Lord.

Jesus tells us the second reason we are not to judge others in this manner, "For with what judgment you judge, you will be judged; and with the measure you use, it will be measured back to you" (Matthew 7:2). We will be judged with that exact same standard.

Paul writes, "Who are you to judge another's servant? To his own master, he stands or falls. Indeed, he will be made to stand, for God is able to make him stand." (Romans 14:4). Who made us the judge to judge in this way?

If we go about with a self-righteous attitude toward others, judging them to condemnation and suggesting no hope for them, claiming they're beyond salvation and the grace of God and should be condemned, we are in essence heaping up judgment upon ourselves. That same standard applies to us. Therefore, we need to be careful about how we handle someone else's flesh lest the same judgment returns to us in the same way. If we judge by a standard that the Lord forbids, then we have taken a role God never intended for us.

Many times, the root of this type of behavior of judging others to condemnation can be a byproduct of jealousy, envy, or pride. We are envious of another and judge their motives. When we pass judgment because a person isn't doing something the way we think they should, we are making a judgment call only God is supposed to make. Only

God knows a person's motives. At best, we are poor judges of the heart.

James puts it this way, "Do not speak evil of one another, brethren. He who speaks evil of a brother and judges his brother, speaks evil of the law and judges the law. But if you judge the law, you are not a doer of the law but a judge. There is one Lawgiver, who is able to save and to destroy. Who are you to judge another?" (James 4:11-12).

It's vital for us to obey His command not to judge others. Jesus assures us we won't escape judgment if we judge others, and He warned His disciples, "with the measure you use, it will be measured back to you."

The rabbis taught the people that God judges a person by two measures: justice and mercy. We may ask ourselves the standard we want others to apply to us: mercy or justice? The Bible says, "Blessed are the merciful for they shall obtain mercy" (Matthew 5:7). If we don't show mercy, then we will not be on the receiving end of mercy, and all of us need God's mercy. "Through the Lord's mercies, we are not consumed, because His compassions fail not. They are new every morning; great is Your faithfulness" (Lamentations 3:22-23).

It is amazing how at times we are critical of others when we see our sins in the life of another. We see others' faults cut and dry while viewing our faults as part of the process of sanctification. In some way, when we see our faults in others, and we judge ourselves vicariously without repentance. At that moment, we feel self-righteous in some carnal way. A Scottish theologian by the name of A. B. Bruce wrote in The Training of the Twelve, "Censoriousness is a Pharisaic vice: that of exalting ourselves by disparaging others, a very cheap way of attaining moral superiority."

King David struggled with this, and after he had committed adultery with Bathsheba followed by the murder of her husband, he lived for a year in deception. The Lord knew about this, and David was miserable until Nathan, the prophet, came to David and told him the story of a man in his kingdom (2 Samuel 12:1-4).

In a moment of rage and anger, David declared the man in question must be put to death! But Nathan then told David he was the man in the story. David had judged his sin in someone else with a heavy hand. Jesus told the story of a Pharisee and tax collector who went to the temple to pray (Luke 18:9-14).

Jesus told this parable to show that people who trust in themselves as righteous despise others. We learn we need to be merciful with other people because we need just as much mercy as others, if not more. Therefore, if we are going to err, let us be those who err on the side of grace and mercy rather than in judgment. Jesus said, "Judge not, and you shall not be judged. Condemn not, and you shall not be condemned. Forgive, and you will be forgiven. Give, and it will be given to you: good measure, pressed down, shaken together, and running over will be put into your bosom. For with the same measure that you use, it will be measured back to you" (Luke 6:37-38).

We are not to put ourselves in the position of ultimate judge, judging others to condemnation, or we will be judged in the same manner. We are not to go around pointing out everybody else's sins. Conversely, this does not mean we are never to judge, never called upon to go to a brother or sister who has stumbled into sin or to those who are backslidden to reason with them. We are to judge others with wisdom discerning the truth.

The Bible tells us to mark those who cause division in the body of Christ and to separate ourselves from them. If a brother or sister errs in the way, we should go to them lovingly and graciously to restore them but never to condemn them. To further illustrate this point, Jesus gave a practical example in the form of a question.

"And why do you look at the speck in your brother's eye, but do not consider the plank in your own eye? Or how can you say to your brother, 'Let me remove the speck from your eye', and look, a plank is in your own eye? Hypocrite! First, remove the plank from your own eye, and then you will see clearly to remove the speck from your brother's eye" (Matthew 7:3-5).

The definition of a speck and a plank differ in size. The Greek word for *speck* is *karphos* meaning a small particle, as a splinter of straw or wood. Some definitions say a speck is like sawdust, which comes from a plank. In the above parable, one man has dust in his eye while the other has a beam protruding from his eye. Though the speck and the plank are made from the same material, the man with the plank in his eye is focused on a mere speck in another's eye. The man with the plank is so busy trying to remove dust from the other person's eye, he fails to see the plank blinding him to his own issues.

Jesus says before attempting to help other people, first deal with your own issues. It is easy to see sin in somebody else's life and to quickly analyze and critically judge others, especially if we struggle with the very same thing. The the Bible tells us, "Therefore you are inexcusable, O man, whoever you are who judge, for in whatever you judge another you condemn yourself; for you who judge practice the same things" (Romans 2:1).

We play a one-stringed instrument all day when we point to faults in others despite the fact we have the exact same problem. Pointing to our sins in another takes the heat off us and acts as a cover or cloak for our own vices. We can project a judgmental attitude onto others making a huge mountain out of a molehill. The disciples struggled with this openly debating who was the greatest among them and they lived with Jesus for three years. In fact, this discussion went on until the day before the crucifixion.

There even came a point when James and John invited their mother to bow before Jesus to ask Him for the opportunity for her sons to sit on His right and left hand in glory. What mother doesn't want the best for her boys? But Jesus told her those positions in heaven were not His to give (Matthew 20:23). When the other ten disciples became upset by the audacity of James and John, Jesus taught the disciples a lesson in humility (Matthew 20:24-28).

It is possible the other disciples saw their sin in James and John and may have been angry they hadn't invited their mothers to approach Jesus in the same manner. Upon hearing Jesus' response, they immediately judged James and John. We may become aware of what is going on in someone else's life while remaining unaware of our own sins, but the Bible tells us to act on the instructions given to us in the Word: "But be doers of the word, and not hearers only, deceiving yourselves. For if anyone is a hearer of the word and not a doer, he is like a man who looks intently at his natural face in a mirror. For he looks at himself and goes away and at once forgets what he was like" (James 1:22-24 ESV).

It's clear Jesus does not condemn criticism per se but rather the criticism of others when comparable self-criticism is not exercised. Often, we know what a person in our lives is supposed to do and we don't mind telling them, whether they need to hear it or not. However, the question is: Are we doing what we are supposed to be doing? It is wise to apply self-criticism before approaching another person. Look at yourself in the mirror and see if this reflects what God's Word says about parameters with respect to judging others. Those parameters begin with us.

To minister in the church, the apostle Paul told Timothy to first check that he applies the doctrine to his own life: "Take heed to yourself and to the doctrine. Continue in them, for in doing this you will save both yourself and those who hear you" (1 Timothy 4:16).

The Bible instructs us to work out our own salvation with fear and trembling and Jesus gives us the balance when he says, "Hypocrite! First, remove the plank from your own eye, and then you will see clearly to remove the speck from your brother's eye" (Matthew 7:5). In other words, stop any hypocritical judgment of others and take care of your own matters. First, repent of what is going on in your own life for the right heart and attitude and after receiving God's mercy, the intention to help another won't be self-righteous but merciful and graceful.

Think about what F. B. Meyer said, "When you see a brother or sister in sin remember this: First of all, we don't know how hard he or she has tried not to sin; second, we don't know the power of the forces that have assailed them; third, we don't know what we would've done if we were in the very same circumstance."

The psalmist put it this way: "Create in me a clean heart, O God, and renew a right spirit within me. Cast me not away from your presence, and take not your Holy Spirit from me. Restore to me the joy of your salvation, and uphold me with a willing spirit. Then I will teach transgressors your ways, and sinners will return to you" (Psalm 51:10-13 ESV).

If we are to confront sin or error in another person's life, there is a proper way to proceed. We must examine our own heart before the Lord, considering our motives. We must go to our brother or sister in humility with the goal of and commitment to the work of restoration. When there is a right heart in us and we are upheld by a generous spirit with the joy of His salvation, then we are in the position to help others. Jesus foretold Peter of his denial and asked him to strengthen the others after he repented: "And the Lord said, "Simon, Simon! Indeed, Satan has asked for you, that he may sift you as wheat. But I have prayed for you, that your faith should not fail; and when you have returned to Me, strengthen your brethren" (Luke 22:31-32).

Peter's discipleship program with Jesus gave him a leadership role. He was more adamant than the others about a willingness to die for the Lord and he was sure there was no way he would ever deny Christ. However, after Peter denied Jesus and the rooster crowed, he wept bitterly and was restored privately, as Paul tells us in 1 Corinthians 15, and publicly, according to John's gospel. From that moment forward, Peter was different, humble, and able to restore others as he had been restored. Those who have failed and been forgiven are far more compassionate and gracious toward others who have also failed.

In Galatians 6, the Bible tells us: "Brethren, if a man is overtaken in any trespass, you who are spiritual restore such a one in a spirit of gentleness, considering yourself lest you also be tempted." We must take note of who we are, where we came from and what God has delivered us from. We must consider how gracious and merciful He is toward us. This is the only way we can honor the Lord and minister to others in a helpful way. If we are not willing to go down the road of restoration, then we should not jump in and get involved. If we are unwilling to see a person reconciled and restored, and only want to intercede for the sake of confrontation, then we need to abstain from helping.

It's imperative we first examine our own hearts before the Lord with the goal of restoration on our minds and in our hearts.

20

CASTING PEARLS

"Do not give dogs what is holy, and do not throw your pearls before pigs, lest they trample them underfoot and turn to attack you" (Matthew 7:6 ESV).

Sometimes people reject the Gospel. We may present the plan of salvation to someone who rejects what we have to share about Jesus. They may mock God and even blast us for sharing. When we realize we cannot take what is holy and throw it at someone who does not want to receive the message but wants to trample upon the Word of God and even blaspheme the name of Jesus Christ, we need to move on before becoming trapped in a confrontational debate. We are not to let people trample upon that which is holy.

Jesus instructs us to move on and not to cast the precious pearls of the Gospel before swine to be trampled upon because it will be a waste of time; we can pray for those who oppose Him and let the Lord deal with them. In Luke 9:5, Jesus instructed the twelve on how to treat rejection of the Gospel: "And whoever will not receive you, when you go out of that city, shake off the very dust from your feet as a testimony against them."

Shake it off! Let God deal with those who want to argue and who don't want to receive the message of salvation.

The apostle Paul also adhered to this principle in his ministry and missionary efforts. When Paul and Barnabas went on their first missionary journey, and the Jews were contradicting their preaching in Antioch, Paul switched gears.

"On the next Sabbath, almost the whole city came together to hear the word of God. But when the Jews saw the multitudes, they were filled with envy; and contradicting and blaspheming, they opposed the things spoken by Paul. Then Paul and Barnabas grew bold and said, 'It was necessary that the word of God should be spoken to you first; but since you reject it, and judge yourselves unworthy of everlasting life, behold, we turn to the Gentiles'" (Acts 13:44-46).

Because the Jews were contentious and did not want to hear what Paul and Barnabas were preaching, they walked away from the Jews and preached salvation to the Gentiles. The Gentiles responded to the Gospel, and churches were planted (Acts 13:42-49).

But when the Jews stirred up trouble in the community again against Paul and Barnabas, the two moved on to the next location. "But the Jews stirred up the devout and prominent women and the chief men of the city, raised up persecution against Paul and Barnabas, and expelled them from their region. But they shook off the dust from their feet against them and came to Iconium" (Acts 13:50-51).

A similar situation "happened in Corinth on the second missionary journey. When the Jews opposed and reviled him, Paul 'shook out his garments' and said to them: 'Your blood be upon your own heads; I am clean. From now on I will go to the Gentiles'" (Acts 18:6).

In this day and age, people do not want to hear about Jesus, and some may become violently opposed. So, what is our recourse? Do we enter into a shouting match with them? No. That wouldn't honor God. Instead, we move on and pray for them.

21

A-S-K: ASK, SEEK, KNOCK

"Ask, and it will be given to you; seek, and you will find; knock, and it will be opened to you" (Matthew 7:7).

What an incredible invitation from the Lord! As we ask, seek and knock, the Lord promises that the door will open to us. As His children, we are guaranteed access into the presence of the Lord, Who sits on the throne of grace, and we can approach Him from anywhere, anytime for anything. The Lord invites us in; He is never too busy to hear from His children.

God is accessible twenty-four hours a day, seven days a week. In fact, in Isaiah, the Lord beckons us to call upon Him: "Ho! Everyone who thirsts, come to the waters; and you who have no money, come, buy and eat. Yes, come, buy wine and milk without money and without price ... Seek the Lord while He may be found, call upon Him while He is near" (Isaiah 51:1, 6).

The Lord invites us to call upon Him. Jesus showed people His open-door policy and extended a constant invitation to seek Him: "Come to me, all who labor and are heavy laden, and I will give you rest. Take my yoke upon you, and learn from me, for I am gentle and lowly in heart, and you will find rest for your souls. For my yoke is easy, and my burden is light" (Matthew 11:28-30 ESV).

We can approach the throne and present our needs anytime, but how many of us take advantage of Jesus' offer? Is He our first or our last resort? We should make Him our first priority to come before Him to ask, seek, and knock. His very words imply continuing to ask, seek, and knock because the Bible says to pray without ceasing. "The effective, fervent prayer of a righteous man avails much" (James 5:16).

Prayer was an essential part of the ministry of the early church. When they needed direction, they prayed; in need of protection, they prayed; for provision, they prayed; for intervention, they prayed. They kept themselves in prayer for boldness to preach in the face of adversity.

Prayer is a consistent continuation of petitioning the Lord, but sometimes that entails waiting on Him. If the Lord says, "wait," then we wait in prayer. We don't have to stop asking until the Lord answers our prayer one way or the other. If the Lord responds with a "No," then it's "No," but if He has us in a waiting hold, then we can continue to petition Him on the matter.

Of course, most of us love when the Lord answers "yes" to our requests, and though it can be difficult when His answer is "no," when He says, "wait," that tests our faith more. It's hard to wait on the Lord but just because God hasn't answered yet doesn't mean He will not answer us. "Elijah was a man with a nature like ours, and he prayed earnestly that it would not rain, and it did not rain on the land for three years and six months. And he prayed again, and the heaven gave rain, and the earth produced its fruit" (James 5:18).

As Elijah petitioned the Lord for rain from Mount Carmel, Elijah had his servant check the weather seven times. He stayed on that mountain praying until the servant returned with a report that he spotted a cloud the size of a man's fist. That was all the proof Elijah needed to come down off the mountain. The Lord had answered his prayers (1 Kings 18:42-45).

The Bible says Elijah was a man of like passions who, like us, consistently sought the Lord in prayer. Elijah serves as an example for us to pray without ceasing (1 Thessalonians 5:17) and with consistency. There is power in prayer and also a promise attached to the Lord's invitation to pray. "For everyone who asks receives, and he who seeks finds, and to him who knocks it will be opened" (Matthew 7:8).

E. M. Pounds, a pastor around the American Civil War era, often quoted early eighteenth-century minister Edward Payson, whose ministry was founded on prayer: "Prayer is the first thing, the second thing and the third thing necessary to a minister. Pray then, my dear brother, pray, pray."

Good advice for all of us.

Notice what Jesus says in Matthew 7:9-11: "Or what man is there among you who, if his son asks for bread, will give him a stone? Or if he asks for a fish, will he give him a serpent? If you then, being evil, know how to give good gifts to your children, how much more will your Father who is in heaven give good things to those who ask Him!"

Once again, Jesus uses the example of reasoning to express the lesser to the greater. If we, as flawed and imperfect parents, love to give good gifts to our children, how much more will He give to those who ask Him? If our children are hungry, we will provide food; our Father in heaven loves to give good gifts to us the same way we love to bless our children. God loves and cares for His children, and the Bible tells us He gives us good things.

Though we may not like or want to receive some things God deems as good for us, His gifts are life-giving and meaningful. It's important to understand that the Lord loves us. It's crucial for us to trust in the Lord and to wait on Him. Another verse that speaks of the good gifts the Lord has in store for us elaborates on spiritual gifts: "If you then, being evil, know how to give good gifts to your children, how much more will your heavenly Father give the Holy Spirit to those who ask Him!" (Luke 11:13).

As His children, we have a history with God. We have seen Him work in our lives, and we can trust that He will continue to work in our lives. "He who began a good work in us will be faithful to complete it until the day of the Lord" (Philippians 1:6).

God knows what we need even before we ask Him.

The Lord said that we should always pray and not lose heart. We are to lift up holy hands without wrath or doubting. The Lord can help us to pray in faith-based upon the promises of His Word. In so many of God's servants, from Abraham to Moses, Joshua to David, even to Jesus, we know that in the waiting, there was more work to be done.

22

THE GOLDEN RULE

"Therefore, whatever you want men to do to you, do also to them, for this is the Law and the Prophets" (Matthew 7:12).

Many have referred to this passage as the "Golden Rule," the "Royal Law," and the "Incomparable Summary." Within the "Sermon on the Mount," Jesus mentions this concept of treating others favorable and in a gracious way. "Give to him who asks you, and from him who wants to borrow from you do not turn away" (Matthew 5:42).

In that same chapter, Jesus said, "But I say to you, love your enemies, bless those who curse you, do good to those who hate you, and pray for those who spitefully use you and persecute you" (v. 44).

Notice the "Golden Rule" begins with the word "therefore," which is used as a conjunction and points back to what Jesus said previously and then connects those previous thoughts with Matthew 7:12. Seemingly, in this sermon, Jesus said the "Golden Rule" could connect to many things. In the immediate context of Matthew 7:1, "Judge not, that you be not judged. For with what judgment you judge, you will be judged; and with the measure you use, it will be measured back to you."

Therefore, "in light of" Matthew 7:1, we could tie that concept into the "Golden Rule," which states: "whatever you want me to do to you, do also to them, for this is the law and the prophets." Phillips Translation reads thus: "Treat other people exactly as you would like to be treated by them. This is the essence of all true religion."

This statement from Jesus is similar to comments made by others who came before Him. From rabbinical writings to Greek and Roman writings, and even in Hinduism and Buddhism, each has its version of this particular principle. For example, Confucius said, "Do not to others what you would not wish done to yourself."

Socrates said, "What stirs your anger when done to you by others that do not do to others."

From Aristotle, "We bear ourselves toward others, and we would desire that they should bear themselves toward us."

According to Hinduism, "This is the sum of duty: Do not do to others what would cause pain if done to you."

"Hurt not others in ways that you yourself would find hurtful," said Buddha.

Moving into the rabbinical writings, the doctor of the law during the time of King Herod, Rabbi Hillel, wrote, "What is hateful to you, do not do to your neighbor. This is the whole Torah; all the rest is commentary. Go and learn it."

While all of these statements seem similar to what Jesus is saying, there is a vast difference. In the past, these religious and philosophical leaders were, in essence, saying stand still and do not do what you don't want others to do to you. In other words, the motive behind what they were saying was to hold back from hurting another so as not to allow another to hurt them. They were concerned with self-preservation, but what Jesus states is radically distinctive from what others said previously. These men stated this precept in the negative and in the passive; whereas, Jesus is stating this principle in the positive and in the active. Jesus goes beyond passive restraint to active benevolence, and the motivation for what Jesus states is based on love and with concern for others. He is saying to love others as we would like to be loved, talk about others the way we would like to be spoken of, and treat others the way we would like to be treated. But He adds we are to treat others this way even if others do not reciprocate the same treatment and concern toward us.

This positive initiative given by Jesus is the opposite of what we would naturally think or practice. The entire "Sermon on the Mount" is contradictory to our natural tendencies and is the opposite of the world's standards, but Jesus called His disciples to follow these principles. Apart from the Spirit of God, which is supernatural, most people would not be compelled to bless those who mistreat them. Blessing those who do not do as we would have them do toward us is what makes a Christian different from everybody else. The "Golden Rule" lived out, differentiates us from the world.

All that said, we can be thankful that keeping the "Golden Rule" is not a prerequisite to salvation because we could never keep this rule perfectly. However, through the work of the Holy Spirit in our lives, we can apply this standard toward other people.

TESTING THE GOLDEN RULE

We can test the "Golden Rule" in our lives by asking ourselves, in a given situation, whether the action we are about to carry out or what we are about to say, is beneficial to the other person and if we would want to receive that same action. In these terms, our speech, thoughts, and actions may change from doing something we might later regret.

Jesus said when this principle is applied and put into practice, it hinges on the entire Old Testament, "for this is the law and the prophets" (Matthew 7:12). This familiar phrase is mentioned more than once in the New Testament and, in fact, is mentioned twice in the "Sermon on the Mount." In Matthew 5:17, Jesus says, "Do not think that I came to destroy the Law or the Prophets. I did not come to destroy but to fulfill."

JESUS GAVE FURTHER INSIGHT into what the law and the prophets meant when later on a scribe tested Him about the first commandment.

> But when the Pharisees heard that he had silenced the Sadducees, they gathered together. And one of them, a lawyer, asked him a question to test him. "Teacher, which is the great commandment in the Law?"
> And he said to him, "You shall love the Lord your God with all your heart and with all your soul and with all your mind. This is the great and first commandment. And a second is like it: You shall love your neighbor as yourself. On these two commandments depend all the Law and the Prophets." (Matthew 22:34-40 ESV).

The law and the prophets is a reference to the Old Testament. Jesus condenses the entire Old Testament into a single principle.

Naturally, we are lovers of ourselves, and the command uses our human flaw as a place to start in how to treat others. We can begin to love people as we love ourselves. Paul said something similar in writing to the Ephesians, comparing a husband's love for his wife to the way Christ loves His church and giving practical advice on marriage (Ephesians 5:25-29).

When the Holy Spirit begins to produce the love of God in our lives, the fruit of the work of the Holy Spirit enables us to go beyond our natural capacity to love. If we then actively apply this principle and treat others the way we would like to be treated, we would see a difference in our culture, within our homes and workplaces, in the church and the world.

As we let the "Golden Rule" sink in, memorizing the words of Jesus, and allowing His words to shine into our own lives, we will realize that we fall short. The "Golden Rule" is a principle we all need to have the Holy Spirit work into our lives, with the end goal of treating others as we desire to be treated.

While it is easy to slip into treating others poorly because they treated us poorly, it's important not to misunderstand the passage. Some may think, "They did it unto me, so I'm going to do it unto them!" But, that's not what the Bible says. Jesus says this differently. He reminds us that loving others is a mark of true Christianity, "A new commandment I give to you, that you love one another; as I have loved you, that you also love one another. By this, all will know that you are My disciples if you have love for one another" (John 13:34-35).

John wrote: "If someone says, "I love God," and hates his brother, he is a liar; for he who does not love his brother whom he has seen, how can he love God whom he has not seen? And this commandment we have from Him: that he who loves God must love his brother also" (1 John 4:20-21).

If we allow this passage to search our hearts, the Holy Spirit can convict us of any hate we justify toward another person, and He can replace that hate with His love. We may think an enemy deserves to be hated, but when we stop and think of what the Lord did for us, we can ask the Lord to extend His love toward that person through us.

23

THE NARROW PATH

"Enter by the narrow gate; for wide is the gate and broad is the way that leads to destruction, and there are many who go in by it. Because narrow is the gate and difficult is the way which leads to life, and there are few who find it" (Matthew 7:13-14).

T hroughout this sermon, Jesus has been comparing the true righteousness of a disciple and follower of Christ to the religious leaders. Jesus now presents a choice for those who are listening. Choosing one way over another is a valid application in light of all Jesus has said up to this point.

What will His hearers choose for themselves? Will they choose external righteousness that profits nothing as they have observed in the religious leaders, or will they desire the righteousness of Christ?

Jesus gives His audience two options. He will present two paths and mention two creeds. He will talk about two types of people and then about two foundations. As we examine the two standards of living Jesus presents, we can determine which path to take. Jesus tells us there is a wide gate that leads to a Broad Road and a narrow gate that leads to the Narrow Path.

WIDE GATE & BROAD ROAD

Jesus tells us the majority of people enter the wide gate that leads to destruction. The Broad Road represents the world and encompasses all belief systems with no curbs and no boundaries. Everybody gets on "Tolerance Highway" to parade down the broad path of human achievement. If there were a sign on the wide gate, it would say, "You can enter here if you're a good person," or "Tolerant people only allowed on this road," or "There is no life after death, all roads lead to God," and the list goes on. The problem with the Broad Road is at the last stop. Those who take this road do not realize their final destination.

The Bible tells us those who get on the Broad Road are headed for ultimate destruction. Maybe not right away. The first part of the journey may be awesome because it may appear like everybody in their world has chosen this road! They can see Jesus on the Narrow Path, but the Broad Road is more appealing! It's so enjoyable! However, as they progress further down this wide road, the realization registers that the Broad Road is leading them to destruction. This once pleasant path is getting them further and further away from God. Throughout history, the pattern of this world has opposed God.

Sin is pleasurable for a season. The Bible says the way of the transgressor is hard, difficult, and painful. Again, maybe not right away, but eventually and eternally. We look around the world today and observe what is happening in our culture and can easily discern the very Broad Road Jesus spoke of, but there is another road.

THE NARROW ROAD

Jesus gives a command: "Enter by the narrow gate ... because narrow is the gate and difficult is the way which leads to life, and there are few who find it."

If we choose to walk on this road with Christ, He tells us upfront: it's narrow, and it's not easy. We enter through a narrow gate, which is no walk in the park. While the Broad Road is also difficult, when we take the Narrow Path, we enter a spiritual battlefield. When the disciples chose to walk this road with Jesus, they went through persecution, hardship, and difficulties because of their identification with Christ. And when we walk on this road, the world will hate us and not speak well of us, either. Some people don't want to travel on the Narrow Path because they don't want others to brand them as "narrow."

But Jesus said this road is narrow! When someone accuses a Christian of narrowness, they can quote Jesus. Those who don't want the world to categorize or demonize them take a different path. However, once a person identifies with Jesus Christ on the Narrow Path, the world is the first to demonize them for their beliefs, calling them bigots or insensitive and intolerant. That's not easy.

Some Christians want to walk on the Narrow Path but don't want others to know. So, they keep one foot on the Broad Road and the other foot on the Narrow Path. They walk both roads so as not to offend the world. The Narrow Path is difficult, but it is the path that leads to eternal life.

We can feel pressure from society on this Narrow Path, and sometimes we can feel all alone. But, it's better to be on the Narrow Path with Jesus that leads to eternal life than on the Broad Road with the rest of the world, which leads to destruction. In light of this, we have to choose one road or the other. The psalmist described the benefits of the Road to Eternity.

> Blessed *is* the man
> Who walks not in the counsel of the ungodly,
> Nor stands in the path of sinners,
> Nor sits in the seat of the scornful;
> But his delight *is* in the law of the Lord,
> And in His law he meditates day and night (Psalm 1:1-2).

THE PROGRESSION ALONG THE BROAD ROAD begins by walking in the counsel of the ungodly. Whoever steps on that path moves from walking to standing with sinners, which is followed by sitting in the comfortable seat of the scornful where a person on this journey becomes part of the crowd. Conversely, the person who walks in the narrow way delights in the law of the Lord and meditates upon His Word day and night.

The Bible tells us in Proverbs 14:12, "There is a way that seems right to a man, but its end is the way of death."

In walking on the path of this world, people accept the base and corrupt standard of the world. They order their behavior according to the patterns of the world, and to them, the Narrow Path seems restrictive and less than standard in size. But the Bible tells us, "Nor is there salvation in any other, for there is no other name under heaven given among men by which we must be saved" (Acts 4:12).

And so the way to eternity is narrow. "For there is one God, and there is one mediator between God and men, the man Christ Jesus, who gave himself as a ransom for all, which is the testimony given at the proper time" (1 Timothy 2:5-6 ESV). Those who journey on the Broad Road can reset their GPS to take the next exit to the Narrow Path before it is too late.

24

FALSE PROPHETS

Here Jesus warns us concerning false prophets: "Beware of false prophets, who come to you in sheep's clothing but inwardly are ravenous wolves. You will recognize them by their fruits. Are grapes gathered from thornbushes, or figs from thistles? So, every healthy tree bears good fruit, but the diseased tree bears bad fruit. A healthy tree cannot bear bad fruit, nor can a diseased tree bear good fruit. Every tree that does not bear good fruit is cut down and thrown into the fire. Thus you will recognize them by their fruits" (Matthew 7:15-20 ESV).

When we read through the Bible, we discover there are many false prophets, such as Balaam, who was given a diviner's fee to manipulate God into cursing His people. When his compromises failed, his false doctrine caused the Israelites to sin (Numbers 22-24; Revelation 2:14).

In Deuteronomy, Moses warned the people about following false prophets who follow other gods over listening to the Voice of the Lord. "But the prophet who presumes to speak a word in My name, which I have not commanded him to speak, or who speaks in the name of other gods, that prophet shall die" (Deuteronomy 18:20).

Jeremiah dealt with a false prophet named Hananiah, who preached the exact opposite of true prophecy, thus deceiving the people.

"Hananiah the son of Azur the prophet, who was from Gibeon, spoke to me in the house of the Lord in the presence of the priests and of all the people, saying, 'Thus speaks the Lord of hosts, the God of Israel, saying: 'I have broken the yoke of the king of Babylon. Within two full years, I will bring back to this place all the vessels of the Lord's house, that Nebuchadnezzar king of Babylon took away from this place and carried to Babylon'" (Jeremiah 28:1-3).

Within the same chapter, this wolf in sheep's clothing removed the yoke off Jeremiah's neck and broke it, then falsely declaring something the Lord never said. "And Hananiah spoke in the presence of all the people, saying, "Thus says the Lord: 'Even so I will break the yoke of Nebuchadnezzar king of Babylon from the neck of all nations within the space of two full years.' And the prophet Jeremiah went his way" (vv. 10-11).

But the Lord intervened by sending His Word to Jeremiah to speak truth to Hananiah. "Then the prophet Jeremiah said to Hananiah the prophet, "Hear now, Hananiah, the Lord has not sent you, but you make this people trust in a lie. Therefore, thus says the Lord: 'Behold, I will cast you from the face of the earth. This year you shall die because you have taught rebellion against the Lord" (vv. 15-16). Jeremiah lamented over false prophets in Jeremiah 23, to which the Lord responded:

> Thus says the Lord of hosts:
> 'Do not listen to the words of the prophets who prophesy
> to you.
> They make you worthless;
> They speak a vision of their own heart,
> Not from the mouth of the Lord' (v. 16).

> "Therefore behold, I am against the prophets," says the Lord,
> "who steal My words every one from his neighbor. Behold,
> I am against the prophets," says the Lord, "who use their

tongues and say, 'He says.' Behold, I am against those who
prophesy false dreams," says the Lord, "and tell them, and
cause My people to err by their lies and by their recklessness.
Yet I did not send them or command them; therefore, they
shall not profit this people at all," says the Lord (vv. 30-32).

Jesus tells us that false prophets can be hard to detect because
they disguise themselves as wolves in sheep's clothing but inwardly
are ravenous wolves. They wear the sheep's suit, but underneath the
clothing resides an entirely different animal. Like a ravenous wolf,
these false prophets seek to devour anyone who will listen to them.
They do and say all the right things and act religious, but their
Christian platform has a hidden agenda. A false prophet is not what
they appear to be. Their Christianity is a façade.

HOW CAN A BELIEVER RECOGNIZE FAKE SHEEP
IF THEY APPEAR FAMILIAR?

First of all, it is easy to detect a fake believer by their diet. Sheep
don't eat sheep. But the top thing on the menu for a wolf is sheep!
One way to detect a fake is when we see people in the body of Christ
devoured and affected by a particular person or group of people in
a negative or hurtful way. We can tell if a false prophet is affecting
sheep by what they are feeding the sheep and then what the sheep are
seeking.

Jesus gives us other ways to identify a wolf in sheep's clothing: by
observing the fruit of someone's life and their ministry because Jesus
said, "You will know them by their fruits." And Jesus follows up this
statement with a question. We could ask: "Do you get good fruit from
a bad tree?" or "Do you get bad fruit from a good tree?" We need
to look at what sort of fruit is coming from their lives. Is their life
producing healthy fruit? Is their fruit a blessing? We can determine a
false prophet from amongst the sheep by their fruit.

Jesus speaks of "fruit" in the spiritual context; the Bible talks about the fruits of the Spirit. Is the fruit of their life affecting people in a good way or is the fruit of their life having a negative impact on people in the body of Christ? We can detect a false prophet by observing the impact of their life and ministry.

FRUITS OF THE SPIRIT VERSUS FRUITS OF THE FLESH

On the other hand, when a person walks in the Spirit, the fruits of the Spirit are evident. We must examine what is coming forth from a person's life to determine genuineness. Jesus warns we will know whether a person is genuine or fake by their fruit. He said, "I am the vine, you are the branches. He who abides in Me, and I in him, bears much fruit; for without Me you can do nothing. If anyone does not abide in Me, he is cast out as a branch and is withered; and they gather them and throw them into the fire, and they are burned. If you abide in Me, and My words abide in you, you will ask what you desire, and it shall be done for you. By this My Father is glorified, that you bear much fruit; so you will be My disciples" (John 15:5-8).

If we abide in Christ and His Word, our tree will bear much fruit. This is based upon where we plant our tree, the type of nutrients it receives, and if it's planted in good soil and watered consistently to bear good fruit, a natural byproduct of where our tree roots. And such is the case with the believer in Christ. If we want to bear good fruit in our lives, we must plant ourselves in the Word and fellowship and congregate where we can be watered and nurtured. Over time, we will naturally, though supernaturally, bear fruit that is pleasing to the Lord because of where we planted ourselves.

The opposite is also true. If someone is not planted in the Lord, but planted in the soil of the flesh, they will produce the fruit of the flesh, which is rotten at its core. Rotten fruit is like fruit that sits out for a while and eventually attracts gnats to hover over what was once healthy fruit. These gnats follow the disintegrating fruit to the garbage dump, like a life not planted in the Lord.

There are two types of trees. Is our life producing good fruit, or is our tree disintegrating? The only way to know is to base the answer upon where we are planted. We are known by our fruit, by what we say and where we go. If we are walking with Jesus, there will be evidence of good fruit.

JESUS DECLARES NOT EVERYONE WHO CLAIMS TO KNOW HIM IS KNOWN BY HIM

> "Not everyone who says to me, 'Lord, Lord,' will enter the kingdom of heaven, but the one who does the will of my Father who is in heaven. On that day many will say to me, 'Lord, Lord, did we not prophesy in your name, and cast out demons in your name, and do many mighty works in your name?' And then will I declare to them, 'I never knew you; depart from me, you workers of lawlessness'" (Matthew 7:21-23 ESV).

We learn from these words of Jesus that we would not want Him to place us in this category. We also learn that, for one thing, some will think that everything is fine between them and the Lord. Not only do they claim Jesus as Lord, but they can list a number of things they say they have done in His name. But notice that although they point out and profess to have done things in His name, apparently they did these things of their own accord. Jesus clarifies that only those who have done the will of the Father shall enter the kingdom of heaven and that those who practice lawlessness will need to depart from heaven.

In reality, their lifestyles did not line up with God's will. Those who thought they were right in the Lord were actually practicing lawlessness. Their actual deeds canceled out what they thought they were doing on behalf of the Lord. We live according to what we believe, but if we say we are followers of Christ, but do not the will of the Father, and do not live accordingly, then in effect we do not worship the true Lord, because we are not concerned about the will of God.

The practice of lawlessness is a way of life. We practice something to become better at it. Those who practice lawlessness, meanwhile saying, "Lord, Lord," will be surprised in the day of reckoning. It's serious that people can be self-deceived into thinking they are okay with the Lord when at the same time their life contradicts their walk with Jesus.

Jesus was not addressing a Christian who messes up or sins, because each of our sins and messes up. Jesus is talking about continuing to practice a lifestyle of sin without a practice of ever walking with the Lord. There is a vast difference of stumbling into something and saying, "God, forgive me, I blew it," as opposed to living with no thought of the Lord whatsoever. Make no mistake; those who think their lifestyle is okay when they are not living according to God's will, and who say, "Lord" in the process, Jesus will tell them they practiced lawlessness and did not do the will of the Father.

When a tree is planted correctly, it doesn't have to strain or do "good works" to bear fruit naturally; but a tree that is not properly planted cannot bear good fruit because it doesn't care about the things of the Lord. It's startling to think that some will be turned away at heaven's gates because the Lord will say, "I never knew you." In essence, if they knew Him, they would've done the will of the Father instead of practicing lawlessness.

At the end of our lives, we don't want to hear the Lord say He didn't know us. We want to hear the words, "Well done, good and faithful servant; you have been faithful over a few things, I will make you ruler over many things. Enter into the joy of your lord" (Matthew 25:23).

25

TWO FOUNDATIONS

U p to this point, we can apply everything Jesus taught in the "Sermon on the Mount" once we establish a firm foundation, for we cannot build a house without a foundation. Having compared two gates, two roads, two trees that grow two kinds of fruit and two types of people now Jesus sums the "Sermon on the Mount" with His authority on two foundations.

> "Everyone then who hears these words of mine and does them will be like a wise man who built his house on the rock. And the rain fell, and the floods came, and the winds blew and beat on that house, but it did not fall, because it had been founded on the rock. And everyone who hears these words of mine and does not do them will be like a foolish man who built his house on the sand. And the rain fell, and the floods came, and the winds blew and beat against that house, and it fell, and great was the fall of it" (Matthew 7:24-27 ESV).

Jesus said whoever hears the "Sermon on the Mount" and applies the principles discussed throughout the sermon is like one who decided to build a house on a solid foundation. A structure built on a rock is sustainable, but a weak foundation, no matter how beautiful on the outside, will eventually crumble. Structural experts list at least five reasons for a building collapse: 1) a weak foundation; 2) building materials not strong enough; 3) builders make mistakes in judgment; 4) the load is heavier than expected, and 5) structural strength is untested.

Jesus provides a solid foundation in which to build our house. Those who apply His principles, or building materials, to their lives can expect a strong structure able to withstand the storms Jesus said would come. Rain hits houses built on rock and falls on houses built on sand. But there is a difference: one stands while the other crumbles. If we build our lives on the rock who is Jesus, our house will stand, but if we disregard the Savior by building our lives on sand, which the Lord calls foolish when the rains come, our house will wash away.

This parable represents two types of people: the believer and the non-believer. Both may go through the same circumstances but with different perspectives. Ultimately, one will stand firm while the other falls. In Jesus' estimation, one is wise, the other foolish, and the difference is where they choose to build a foundation for their lives.

The Bible tells us very clearly the rock is Christ! He is the rock, and the Bible calls Him the chief cornerstone, tried and precious. Isaiah wrote: "Therefore thus says the Lord God: 'Behold, I lay in Zion a stone for a foundation, a tried stone, a precious cornerstone, a sure foundation; Whoever believes will not act hastily'" (Isaiah 28:16).

Peter referenced Psalm 118:22 when he wrote: "Therefore it is also contained in the Scripture, 'Behold, I lay in Zion a chief cornerstone, elect, precious, and he who believes on Him will by no means be put to shame'" (1 Peter 2:6). And in Matthew 21:42, "Jesus said, 'Have you never read in the Scriptures: 'The stone which the builders rejected has become the chief cornerstone. This was the Lord's doing, and it is marvelous in our eyes'?"

If we are going to build our lives, marriages, and family on a lasting foundation, we are wise to consider a foundation that is tried and true.

Hardships and difficult days are sure to bring storms into our homes, but with Jesus, our house can stand firm because if we choose to build on Christ and His Word, our lives will stand on a solid foundation.

Even if the world crumbles around us, His foundation is strong and offers solid footing. On the other hand, those who reject Jesus and build their houses on the sands of this world will experience a different outcome. Their gray days will cloud over with storms. Their weak foundation is incapable of withstanding the attacks of the enemy, and they will be left with nothing because of where they chose to build. They will not be able to stand.

> Finally, my brethren, be strong in the Lord and in the power of His might. Put on the whole armor of God, that you may be able to stand against the wiles of the devil. For we do not wrestle against flesh and blood, but against principalities, against powers, against the rulers of the darkness of this age, against spiritual hosts of wickedness in the heavenly places. Therefore, take up the whole armor of God, that you may be able to withstand in the evil day, and having done all, to stand (Ephesians 6:10-13).

THE CONTRAST IS OBVIOUS

> "Therefore, whoever hears these sayings of Mine, and does them, I will liken him to a wise man who built his house on the rock: and the rain descended, the floods came, and the winds blew and beat on that house; and it did not fall, for it was founded on the rock. "But everyone who hears these sayings of Mine, and does not do them, will be like a foolish man who built his house on the sand: and the rain descended, the floods came, and the winds blew and beat on that house; and it fell. And great was its fall" (Matthew 7:24-27).

CONCLUSION

At the conclusion of His "Sermon on the Mount," Jesus presents us with a choice. There are two paths. Jesus walked the narrow road and left us a roadmap to follow leading to eternal life. The devil operates the broad road leading people away to eternal destruction.

Then there are two types of trees, which produce two kinds of fruit. The tree planted in Christ bears good fruit, and the tree planted in this world bears rotten fruit.

Two types of people—those who say Jesus is Lord but live in lawlessness according to the culture, and those who follow Jesus in harmony with His principles. Those who don't follow Jesus will be surprised on the day of judgment, and those who follow Him will be blessed.

And then we have two foundations—the solid rock that stands regardless of what it faces; and the weak foundation that crumbles.

Everyone has to decide which direction to take. No one can make this decision for us. God gives us a free will; for love to be love, there has to be a choice. Love is the highest ethic.

The Lord would never force anyone to go on the Narrow Path. In His "Sermon on the Mount," Jesus gave all the facts and benefits for us to choose. There is a bridge from the Wide Road to the Narrow

Path—the cross of Christ. Jesus died so we could exit that broad road leading us to destruction to enter the narrow gate that leads to life.

Which side do you most identify with and which path are you on? Which way would you most likely choose?

> "And so it was, when Jesus had ended these sayings, that the people were astonished at His teaching, for He taught them as one having authority, and not as the scribes" (Matthew 7:28-29).

FIELD NOTES

FIELD NOTES

REFERENCES

Barclay, William. *The Gospel of Matthew, Volume 1.* Westminster John Knox Press. 2001.

Blue Letter Bible. "O.T. Names of God - Study Resources." https://www.blueletterbible.org/study/misc/name_god.cfm. Accessed 29 May, 2019.

Bruce, A. B. *The Training of the Twelve.* Edinburgh: T. & T. Clark, 38, George Street. 1871.

Greenberg, P.E., et. al. "Economic Burden of Anxiety Disorders." ADAA (Anxiety and Depression Association of America) Journal of Clinical Psychiatry. 1999. https://www.ncbi.nlm.nih.gov/pubmed/10453795 captured May 29, 2019.

Lewis, C. S. *The Weight of Glory.* (New York. Simon & Schuster. 1996), pp. 135-136.

Meyer, F. B. *The Secret of Guidance.* Fleming H. Revell Company. 1896.

Moody, Dwight L. *Prevailing Prayer: What Hinders It?* Fleming H. Revell Company. 1884.

Müller, George. "The beginning of anxiety is the end of faith, and the beginning of true faith is the end of anxiety." Quote. *The Churchmen.* 1897.

National Alliance of Mental Health. "Mental Health by the Numbers." 2017.

National Institute of Mental Health. "Any Mental Illness (AMI) Among Adults" https://www.nimh.nih.gov/health/statistics/mental-illness.shtml#part_154785, captured May 29, 2019.

The New Testament in Modern English by J.B Phillips copyright © 1960, 1972 J. B. Phillips. Administered by The Archbishops' Council of the Church of England. Used by Permission.

Payson, Edward. *A Memoir of the Rev. Edward Payson*. 1830. (See Pounds)

Pounds, E. M. (1835-1913). Quoted Payson: "Prayer is the first thing, the second thing and the third thing necessary to a minister. Pray then, my dear brother, pray, pray."

Robertson, A. T. Quote. "The Sermon on the Mount stands out as the greatest single sermon of all time in its pointedness and power." *Jesus as a Soul Winner*. 1937.

Ryle, J.C. *The Gospel of Matthew: Expository Thoughts on the Gospels.* 1856.

Spurgeon, Charles. Commentary. "The Sermon on the Mount." 1873.

Steverman, Ben. "Millennials Are Causing the U.S. Divorce Rate to Plummet." Bloomberg. Sept. 25, 2018

Stott, John. *Reading the Sermon on the Mount with John Stott*. Intervarsity Press. Aug. 5, 2016.

World Health Organization. "Depression." March 22, 2018. https://www.who.int/news-room/fact-sheets/detail/depression, captured May 29, 2019.

World Health Organization. "Depression and Other Common Mental Disorders: Global Health Estimates." WHO/MSD/MER/2017.2.

CALVARY CHAPEL has been formed as a fellowship of believers in the Lordship of Jesus Christ. Our supreme desire is to know Christ and to be conformed into His image by the power of the Holy Spirit.

For more information, visit: calvarysjc.com.

A DAILY WALK is the radio ministry of Calvary Chapel San Juan Capistrano featuring studies and sermons from Pastor John.

To find your local station, you can visit:
http://www.adailywalk.org/stations

or subscribe to the podcasts at:
https://podcasts.apple.com/us/podcast/a-daily-walk-radio/id816776146.

FOLLOW Pastor John on social media.

Instagram:
@JohnPrandall

Twitter
@pjrandall7

Check out his website here:
https://www.pastorjohnrandall.com/home.

ABOUT THE AUTHOR

John Randall has been in pastoral ministry for over two decades. He served as senior pastor of Calvary Chapel in Brandon, Florida and presently fills the role of senior pastor of Calvary Chapel in San Juan Capistrano.

John is the featured Bible teacher on the national radio broadcast "A Daily Walk." Known for his clear and relatable presentation of the Scriptures, John and his wife Michelle reside in Southern California. They married in 1992 and have four children.